T. S. Eliot on Shakespeare

Studies in Modern Literature, No. 66

A. Walton Litz, General Series Editor

Professor of English
Princeton University

Ronald Bush

Consulting Editor for Titles on T. S. Eliot
Professor of Literature
California Institute of Technology

Other Titles in This Series

T. S. Eliot on Shakespeare

by
Charles Warren

UMI Research
Press

Ann Arbor, Michigan

Extracts from contributions to books, periodicals, etc., are reprinted by permission of Mrs. Valerie Eliot and Faber & Faber Ltd.

Extracts from *Selected Essays* by T. S. Eliot are reprinted by permission of Harcourt Brace Jovanovich and Faber & Faber Ltd.

Extracts from the Clark Lectures at Cambridge and the Shakespeare Lectures at Harvard are reprinted by permission of Mrs. Valerie Eliot and Faber & Faber Ltd.
© Mrs. Valerie Eliot 1987

Extracts from *The Use of Poetry and the Use of Criticism* are reprinted by permission of Harvard University Press and Faber & Faber Ltd.

The author would like to thank the Houghton Library at Harvard University for permission to read and quote from the Shakespeare and Clark lectures.

Produced and distributed by
UMI Research Press
an imprint of
University Microfilms, Inc.
Ann Arbor, Michigan 48106

Library of Congress Cataloging in Publication Data

Warren, Charles, 1948-
T. S. Eliot on Shakespeare.

(Studies in modern literature ; no. 66)
Revision of thesis (Ph.D.)—Princeton University, 1985.
Bibliography: p.
Includes index.
1. Shakespeare, William, 1564-1616—Criticism and interpretation—History—20th century. 2. Eliot, T. S. (Thomas Stearns), 1888-1965—Knowledge—Literature. 3. Shakespeare, William, 1564-1616—Influence—Eliot. I. Title. II. Series.
PR2972.E57W3   1987   822.3'3   86-14658
ISBN 0-8357-1784-4 (alk. paper)

For my mother and father

Contents

Acknowledgments

This book began at Princeton University, and I would like to thank my advisors there, A. Walton Litz and Michael Goldman, for many general and specific suggestions. The following people read considerable portions or all of the manuscript and offered crucial, much appreciated advice: Barbara Lewalski, Stanley Cavell, Gus Blaisdell, and William Pritchard. I would like to thank others for reading previous work of mine on this subject, for helpful conversations about the subject, and for general encouragement of the most important kind while I was at work on this project: Katherine Kimball, James Maraniss, William Rothman, Marian Keane, John Brewer, Jane Burbank, and Huntley Dent.

Introduction

T. S. Eliot is not usually thought of as a Shakespeare critic. But in fact he wrote about Shakespeare continually, and his work presents a developed view of him. This book contains a complete review of Eliot's Shakespeare criticism and presents a number of new ideas about Eliot's thinking.

The sources I draw on begin with two well-known essays on Shakespeare, "Hamlet" and "Shakespeare and the Stoicism of Seneca." I also include other collected writings that contain extended discussions of Shakespeare, such as the "Ben Jonson" and "Massinger" essays and the Norton Lectures, *The Use of Poetry and the Use of Criticism*. But beyond this there is much else, including many uncollected essays in periodicals, introductions to books, and talks for the BBC (published in *The Listener*). These show immediately how far Eliot's interest in Shakespeare went, far beyond what is indicated by the familiar essays. Most important of all the little-known work is a set of two unpublished lectures, "Shakespeare as Poet and Dramatist," given in 1937. When all this is taken into account, a new picture emerges, a picture of Eliot as a great Shakespeare critic.

In his very early essays Eliot refers to Shakespeare repeatedly, attesting to his greatness as an artist and opening specific subjects he will have a good deal to say about later, such as Shakespeare's use of rhetoric and his development. Eliot is often taken to be negative about Shakespeare in the "Hamlet" essay (1919). But I argue that this essay is meant to propose a new standard for the Shakespeare play, and to direct our attention away from *Hamlet* to other parts of the canon, notably *Coriolanus* and *Antony and Cleopatra*.

In the 1920s Eliot goes on to develop an elaborate view of the Shakespeare play. His view involves the use of language, the nature of the created character, the nature of the whole, and the relation of the work to the audience. His discussion of Shakespeare's language makes clear what has not really been appreciated about Eliot's general view of poetry: he proposes not a poetry that is especially good at referring to a recognizable world, but a poetry that creates something anew that we will regard *as if* it were an object. Among Eliot's discussions of the created character is a little-known essay written for Wyndham

Lewis's *Tyro,* where Eliot talks about the way the audience lives out imaginatively the life of the character; here Shakespeare is brought into relation with prose fiction, the cinema, and the music hall. Eliot also speaks in these years of a "poetic vision" that the whole Shakespeare play conveys to the audience. The "poetic vision" involves a large-scale "rhythm" that affects the audience like ritual, and there is a special use of comic and serious moods, of "real" emotion and the "typical." Eliot wrote a review of a production of *King Lear* in *The Criterion* to help make clear his notion of the effect of the play on the audience.

From the middle 1920s through the 1930s Eliot engages in an ongoing discussion about meaning in Shakespeare. This discussion, I would say, is the single most interesting revelation of a look back at all the criticism. In some essays of the middle 1920s Eliot raises doubts about Shakespeare's attitude to life, his intellectual coherence, and even the coherence of his art. Arising from these doubts, in the decade leading up to the 1937 Shakespeare Lectures, Eliot's chief Shakespearean subject becomes the problem of "meaning"—is there in Shakespeare's plays a coherence or unity in dealing with "anarchic" material that redeems this material, so to speak, making the play a valuable *intellectual* presentation? In a little-known essay on Valéry, Eliot begins to posit poetic meaning as an area beyond pure poetic expression and "tending toward," but not *being,* intellectual formulation. This delicate idea is applied to the work of Shakespeare in "Shakespeare and the Stoicism of Seneca" (1927). Here and in other essays of the period Eliot thinks of meaning as the very presentness or thereness of all that is involved in the Shakespeare work. For the material to have become so entirely art amounts to a moral comprehension—though it takes an artist like Shakespeare to compel such a feeling.

In 1930 Eliot wrote an introduction for Wilson Knight's *The Wheel of Fire* that endorses the idea of a substantive "vision" in Shakespeare, something more nearly intellectual than the "poetic vision" of the 1920s discussions. In a good deal of writing going well into the 1930s, Eliot refines this idea of a vision, relating it to all the components of the Shakespeare play. The vision amounts to a perspective, attained as if from beyond life, upon elements that are present in the play. The analogy of listening to a piece of music is used frequently to account for the way the audience comes into contact with Shakespeare's vision. And Eliot speculates a good deal about the way Shakespeare worked his personal concerns, through the mode of a popular art and its special demands, into a universal statement. Here Eliot's discussion of Shakespeare is most important for understanding a central subject in all his criticism, the "transmutation" of life into a work of art of general significance. In 1930–31 Eliot wrote two poems, "Marina" and *Coriolan,* that seem to confirm his new sense of a substantial meaning in Shakespeare, something suitable for recasting into a new poetic work. (Chapter 3 includes a discussion of these poems and reviews Eliot's use of Shakespeare in his earlier poetry.)

Finally, the 1937 Shakespeare Lectures sum up Eliot's thinking about Shakespeare. He offers a picture of Shakespeare's development as concentrating more and more on his vision, which was always implicit in his work, but which comes to direct exposure only in the late plays—a perspective on life as if from beyond life. Eliot comments on a number of the plays in detail— *King John, Romeo and Juliet, Hamlet, Antony and Cleopatra, Pericles*—and discusses general concepts such as the "dramatic" in the usual sense and the "ultra-dramatic" that must be found through the dramatic. The 1937 lectures also seem to relate to the *Four Quartets* (1936–42). There are many terms in common between the two works; I propose that the thinking Eliot did about Shakespeare helped his thinking about life itself, which issued in the writing of the *Quartets*.

Eliot was well aware of other prominent Shakespeare critics of his day. He mentions many of these, including A. C. Bradley, Stoll, Robertson, Middleton Murry, Wyndham Lewis, Wilson Knight, and Granville-Barker. Editor of *The Criterion* (1923–39), Eliot published a good deal of commentary on Shakespeare by others than himself; a list and brief description of all these articles appears in the appendix to this book. But Eliot never aligns himself fully with any critic—he takes points here and there and puts them to his own use, standing alone as a Shakespeare critic. Eliot's criticism is best understood—at least it needs to be so understood *first*—as a system on its own terms. It progressed making use of other thinkers but did so primarily to spell out its own instincts. What Eliot said more than once about the Shakespeare canon, we can say of his own work: it needs to be regarded first as a whole, as having developed along its own lines without accident.

Commentary on Eliot's views on Shakespeare has fallen into several stages and certainly requires a new and thorough account. At every stage Eliot has been regarded only in part. In the early twenties there was controversy about Eliot's critique of *Hamlet;*[1] indeed, the negative aspect of that essay has left the impression with some critics that Eliot simply did not enjoy Shakespeare, that he is an anti-Shakespearean.[2] A second stage of comment, largely developed during the 1930s and 1940s, consists of tributes by prominent writers on Shakespeare who took their own work to be in part a carrying on from Eliot—L. C. Knights, who became in the thirties *The Criterion's* chief writer on Shakespeare; M. C. Bradbrook; Derek Traversi; S. L. Bethell; Henri Fluchère. The gist of these tributes is not that Eliot has given a great deal of detailed comment on Shakespeare to be taken up and thought about; instead it is that he is inspiring in his general lesson in the close reading of poetry, especially Elizabethan-Jacobean poetry, and in his insistence on the importance of convention in Elizabethan drama.[3] At the end of Eliot's life and in the years just after his death, when the trend of Shakespeare criticism was moving away from the Knights-Traversi approach, there appeared articles by Helen Gardner, C. B.

Watson, and G. K. Hunter attacking Eliot and the criticism he inspired for its too great concern with poetic language and symbolic organization, its neglect of realistic character creation, Renaissance heroic values, and the theatrical aspects of the plays.[4] This criticism of Eliot, like the praise of the previous generation, took him simply as a general inspiration for close reading and for thinking along conventional symbolic lines.

In the last two decades, as critics have begun more and more to read Eliot's uncollected prose, they have recognized that he had a considerable interest in Shakespeare throughout his career. Ronald Bush in his recent general study of Eliot, for example, recognizes this important interest and makes special use of the Shakespeare Lectures.[5] Still, recent accounts of Eliot on Shakespeare are rather brief and general except for one. And this longer study, a Canadian Ph.D. dissertation by Sudhakar Marathe, is too purely descriptive of the pieces of Eliot's commentary and their whereabouts; it does not discern the general view that is contained in them.[6]

1

Early Criticism and the "Hamlet" Essay

Intimations of Shakespeare's Greatness, 1917–19

In the earliest years when Eliot was publishing literary criticism, he made numerous references to Shakespeare attesting to his greatness and power, his mastery as an artist, and to the inability of criticism—as we know it, at least—to assimilate him. Eliot does not name critics; he attacks general human unawareness. In addition, Eliot begins to discuss several specific subjects that he will make a great deal of as the years go by: Shakespeare's use of language, his employment of rhetoric for insight into character, his presentation of a "point of view" or "world" as opposed to a "philosophy," and his deliberate experimentation and development from play to play.

In a 1917 review of the letters of J. B. Yeats for the *Egoist* Eliot approves of Yeat's use of Shakespeare as a standard. Yeats wants to show the limits of the moralizing type of mind to be found in Bunyan: "Bunyan would have called Hamlet 'Mr. Facing-Both-Ways,' and Juliet 'Mistress Bold-Face' or 'Carnality,' and Romeo 'Mr. Lovelorn,' and Macbeth 'Mr. Henpecked,' etc., finding where he could epithets to belittle and degrade the temple of human nature and its altars." Eliot himself goes on,

The substance of poetry, Mr. Yeats says, is "truth seen in passion" . . .

> the poet does not seek to be original, but the truth, and to his dismay and consternation, it may be, he finds the original, thereby to incur hostility and misunderstanding.

> Mr. Yeats understands poetry better than any one I have ever known who was not a poet, and better than most of those who have the reputation of poets. This last quotation, in fact, is a thought which takes very deep roots; it strikes through the tangle of literature direct to the subsoil of the greatest—to Shakespeare and Dante and Aeschylus.[1]

One may not rest easily with the dismissal of Bunyan here; but Bunyan is a writer in whom Eliot is very little interested—he will never return to discuss him. The real point in the article is the idea of great poetry, in Shakespeare and elsewhere, as being a momentous *fact,* the finding of an important truth in life and the realization of this truth in powerful art which cannot be labeled or reduced or generalized.

This concept of great art, and in particular of Shakespeare, is one Eliot will stay with and refine throughout his critical career. In other essays of these early years Eliot stresses Shakespeare's power and the need for a direct and open contact with his work, such as criticism tends to avoid, trying instead to make the work comfortable or manageable (as Bunyan *might* be supposed to do with his moralizing epithets). In the *Egoist* "Observations" of 1918, signed "T. S. Apteryx," where Eliot speaks of the need of criticism "to disturb and alarm the public," he says: "England puts her great writers away securely in a Safe Deposit Vault, and curls to sleep like Fafner. There they go rotten . . . We must insist upon the importance of intelligent criticism . . . It is essential that each generation should reappraise everything for itself. Who, for instance, has a first-hand opinion of Shakespeare?"[2] In a piece on "Contemporanea" Eliot praises Wyndham Lewis and Joyce, noting that their work is "terrifying"; Eliot thinks of Shakespeare: "When a work of art no longer terrifies us we may know that we were mistaken, or that our senses are dulled: we ought still to find Othello or Lear frightful." Eliot in his susceptibilities sounds a little like Dr. Johnson, whom he will come to praise in various ways and to feel close to; Eliot's review of Middleton Murry's *Shakespeare* in 1936 says that with Hamlet's speculations on death and the afterlife, "*some* now would be as amazed and terrified as Johnson."[3]

Eliot's fourth *Egoist* article under the heading "Reflections on Contemporary Poetry" speaks of the intimacy that may be obtained with a writer of the past, an intimacy that might enable us to "penetrate . . . the thick and dusty circumlocutions about his reputation." He comments that "probably not one man in each generation is great enough to be intimate with Shakespeare."[4] This does not hold out much hope for criticism; but the size and power of Shakespeare, it seems, are not to be lost sight of, whatever the cost. In his 1919 review of a production of *The Duchess of Malfi,* where he seeks to revive the claims of poetic drama, Eliot begins by noting: "Years of patient labour have so purified, transmogrified, and debased Shakespeare that several of his plays can be produced before audiences of the most civilized householders and shareholders in the world." The problem with criticism and production of both Shakespeare and other Elizabethan drama is that we do not attend to the poetry and the "poetic vision" of the whole, but to what the actor can "make," with his modern psychology, of this or that part. "What survives is a few mutilated good stage plays, out of a large number; actors 'making' parts—Mr. A.'s 'Hamlet,' B.'s 'Shylock,' C.'s 'Richard III,'—the poetry tolerated because overlooked . . . we have seen every Hamlet but Shakespeare's. As 'Hamlet' is performed, only the plot is Shakespeare's; and the words might as well be the flattest prose."[5]

In these years, of course, Eliot is pressing the point that the fully achieved work of art is to be distinguished from the work that is largely just intention or overly "personal." More than once Shakespeare is instanced as the real thing (even in the "Hamlet" essay, where that play is challenged on these grounds of impersonality and being fully achieved, several other plays are mentioned as great successes). In an early article on Kipling Eliot speaks of that writer and Swinburne as being "oratorical." He invokes Shakespeare as the contrast:

> Like the public speaker's, [Kipling's and Swinburnes's] business is not to express, to lay before you, to *state* but to propel, to impose on you the idea. And, like the orator, they are personal: not by revelations, but by throwing themselves in and gesturing the emotion of the moment. The emotion is not "there" simply, coldly independent of the author, of the audience, there and for ever like Shakespeare's and Aeschylus' emotions . . .
>
> I look down at his feet: but that's a fable.
> If that thou be'st a devil, I cannot kill thee,
>
> is "there," cold and indifferent.[6]

"Tradition and the Individual Talent" is the most famous place for this line of discussion, and there too Shakespeare is brought up, again with Aeschylus, and now Dante, as the model for the "transmutation" of emotion into art: "Great variety is possible in the transmutation of emotion: the murder of Agamemnon, or the agony of Othello, gives an artistic effect apparently closer to a possible original than . . . scenes from Dante. In the *Agamemnon,* the artistic emotion approximates to the emotion of an actual spectator; in *Othello* to the emotion of the protagonist himself. But the difference between art and the event is always absolute."[7] In an essay for the *Chapbook* in 1921, "Prose and Verse," Eliot brings up Remy de Gourmont (as he does frequently in these years) and the dictum that style preserves literature. He then cites the Gravediggers scene in *Hamlet* as being "great poetry," along with poems of Donne and Henry King's "Exequy," where a human emotion is "concentrated and fixed."[8] Thus, Shakespeare is not only great and powerful, overwhelming to familiar critical terms, but perfect in his art, "impersonal" and perenially "there."

Shakespeare's use of language is a subject Eliot is already discussing in a variety of ways in these early years. This is the area where a number of critics of the next generation credit Eliot with having made his most momentous contribution to Shakespeare studies; L. C. Knights, M. C. Bradbrook, and others express gratitude to Eliot in introductions to their own work and in retrospectives of earlier twentieth-century criticism.[9] Eliot will have more to say about Shakespeare's language as the years go on, but already in 1917–19 he is beginning to talk about the effect of the language on the imagination of the spectator, the nature of metaphor in Shakespeare, and the confluence of thought and sensuousness. The implication is there, to be enforced by more Eliot will say and to be developed in the criticism of Wilson Knight and others, that the way to confront the powerful Shakespeare, the great artist we have been avoiding, is through close response to his poetry.

In "The Noh and the Image" of 1917, Eliot distinguishes the type of drama where our attention centers in the image presented on the stage, from that, typically Shakespeare's, where we are worked on primarily through the language, the stage image being a little beside the point, a sort of aftereffect to what transpires between the language and the imagination of the spectator.

> The peculiarity of the Noh is that the focus of interest, and centre of construction, is the scene *on the stage*. In reading *Hamlet,* for instance, there is a perfectly clear image of a frosty night, at the beginning; in *Macbeth* there is a clear image of the castle at nightfall where the swallows breed. We imagine these, however, as they would be in reality; in reading the Noh, we have not so much help from our imagination, for the image we wish to form is the image on the stage . . . The English stage is merely a substitute for the reality we imagine.

Eliot later on will not sound antitheatrical in his reading of Shakespeare's dramatic poetry; he will insist on the at-oneness of poetry and dramatic action. But here he is trying to draw a distinction with a very different type of drama, and he will never in fact lose sight of the importance in Shakespeare of the working of the words upon the imagination. The instancing here of the scene from *Macbeth* anticipates the comments on particular lines from this scene and on Shakespeare's "visual imagination" and "sense of place" in the "Milton" essay of 1936. Further on in the "Noh" essay Eliot comments on the imagination of ghosts and the reactions of human characters. In the play "Awoi No Uye" a ghost is enacted, and the dreaming or feverish protagonist (Awoi) is represented by a folded red kimono placed on the stage. "The phantom-psychology of Orestes and Macbeth is as good as that of Awoi; but the method of making the ghost real is different. In the former cases the ghost is given in the mind of the possessed; in the latter case the mind of the sufferer is inferred from the reality of the ghost."[10] In *Macbeth* we may see the ghost of Banquo (as we may see Orestes' Furies), but we know and contemplate the ghost in the postulated mind of the protagonist, which begins for us in the words.

In other comments Eliot shows himself attuned to details of Shakespeare's poetry and the implication of meaning in the style and procedures of the poetry. In "Studies in Contemporary Criticism" (1918), in the midst of a discussion of good and bad metaphors and what good and bad critics are able to recognize, Eliot remarks:

> The healthy metaphor adds to the strength of the language; it makes available some of that physical source of energy upon which the life of language depends.
>
> . . . in her strong toil of grace
>
> is a complicated metaphor which has this effect; and as in most good metaphor, you can hardly say where the metaphorical and the literal meet.[11]

This line from *Antony and Cleopatra* is one Eliot will quote and comment on repeatedly in his career. The idea of merging the literal and metaphorical in Shakespeare, or the idea that the literal is in effect stated *to be* the metaphorical

—that the metaphorical is the realm where we have acquaintance with the literal—is an idea Eliot will press in the important "Massinger" essay and in still later work. Also, Eliot will make more of the idea that physical energy is the means to our involvement in the metaphor, that we are in a sense acted upon by the lines and that our apprehension of whatever significance the lines have to convey consists in this transaction between the lines and ourselves.

In the essay on Swinburne's criticism Eliot notes Swinburne's comparison of Chapman to Jonson and points out that this critic neglects a "quality of the age" Chapman in fact shares more thoroughly with Donne. "The quality in question is not peculiar to Donne and Chapman. In common with the greatest—Marlowe, Webster, Tourneur, and Shakespeare—they had a quality of sensuous thought, or of thinking through the senses, or of the senses thinking, of which the exact formula remains to be defined."[12] Of course, Eliot will do more to try to define this quality. It is notable here that the idea of "thought" being at one with the senses in this poetry, Shakespeare's and others', is close to the idea of the literal being at one with the metaphorical, this at-oneness consisting in an access of "physical energy."

The 1919 "Marlowe" essay is one of Eliot's best and probably most influential essays. It demonstrates that the purpose and overall dramatic form of Marlowe, a certain "serious" farce, is discerned and characterized through close attention to the style of the verse, a certain "hesitating on the edge of caricature." (Indicating this emphasis on the verse, the essay was called "Notes on the Blank Verse of Christopher Marlowe" in its original appearance in *Art and Letters* and in the *Sacred Wood* collection.) Eliot is speaking of a quality akin, he says, to the work of Ben Jonson and very different from Shakespeare. But the very idea that the way to the final purposes of a dramatist lies through attention to the qualities of the verse is a model easily taken up for Shakespeare.

At the end of the "Marlowe" essay Eliot makes a comparison to Shakespeare, suggesting how close attention to Shakespeare's poetry might proceed. He says of the account of the sack of Troy in *Dido* ("At last, the soldiers pull'd her by the heels, / And swung her howling in the empty air . . ."):

> By comparing the whole speech with Clarence's dream, in *Richard III*, one acquires a little insight into the difference between Marlowe and Shakespeare:
>
> > What scourge for perjury
> > Can this dark monarchy afford false Clarence?
>
> There, on the other hand, is what Marlowe's style could not do; the phrase has a concision which is almost classical, certainly Dantesque.[13]

The phrases with epithets, "dark monarchy" and "false Clarence," ask us to stop and think. The unity of sound between "scourge" and "perjury" and then again in "dark monarchy" gives to each of these ideas its own poetic identity. We are momentarily taken into a world with each phrase. And on the word "afford" we have to stop and think, if only for an instant; the word suggests a casualness and uncontrolledness about the punishment given, perhaps more terrible than a full and just attention to the culprit would be. Such is Shakepeare's "concision," very different from Marlowe's speed and his consistent level of caricature over a large area.

What about the comparison here of Shakespeare's "concision" to Dante? Eliot's early essay on Dante is concerned with structure and argues that once the whole poem is read and understood, one sees how the interests and insights of the whole are focused in individual incidents and lines (*SW*, pp. 158–71). The later "Dante" essay (1929) has more to say about particular lines and phrases and gives some sense of the "concision" Eliot must have had in mind in comparing Dante to Shakespeare early on. Dante says of Brunetto Latini in Hell, that he "runs like the winner" among the racers for the green cloth at Verona. And Eliot comments that likening Brunetto to the winner gives a quality of the greatest poetry to the account of the punishment. We are "*hit*" (Eliot's emphasis) by these lines (*SE*, p. 209). Brunetto is inherently like a winner, and he is forced to suffer his punishment while reliving his winner-like quality. There is a complexity about punishment. As with Clarence, we are made to pause and think over a phrase. We go in the "Marlowe" essay from the quality of Marlowe's verse to his larger temperament and purposes, and the suggestion is clear, in the comment on Shakespeare at the end, that we might similarly move from the noticing of poetic detail to the proper consideration of Shakespeare's larger temperament and purposes.

Closely related to the subject of style and detail in Shakespeare's language is that of his use of rhetoric. In the 1919 essay on Rostand, "'Rhetoric' and Poetic Drama," Eliot begins talking about rhetoric in drama in general, asking where is it "right because it issues from what it has to express?" Beginning on a point close to that about Shakespeare's "concision" in the "Marlowe" essay, Eliot says we think of Shakespeare as the dramatist who concentrates everything into a sentence—"Pray you undo this button"; "Honest honest Iago." But in fact there is a rhetoric "proper" to Shakespeare even in the greatest plays:

> The really fine rhetoric of Shakespeare occurs in situations where a character in the play *sees himself* in a dramatic light:
>
> OTHELLO: And say, besides,—that in Aleppo once . . .
> CORIOLANUS: If you have writ your annals true, 'tis there,
>   That like an eagle in a dovecote, I
>   Fluttered your Volscians in Corioli.
>   Alone I did it. Boy!
> TIMON: Come not to me again; but say to Athens,
>   Timon hath made his everlasting mansion
>   Upon the beached verge of the salt flood . . .

There is fine rhetoric too when Enobarbus is inspired to see Cleopatra in such a dramatic light—"The barge she sat in. . . ." And when Antony addresses the crowd in *Julius Caesar,* we concentrate not on the content of his speech—Eliot says *"Bedeutung"*—but on its effect on the crowd and on the working of Antony's mind as he prepares the effect. In all this material we are given "a new clue to the character, in noting the angle from which he views himself."[14]

Years later, in his famous remarks on Othello's last speech in "Shakespeare and the Stoicism of Seneca," Eliot will analyze Shakespeare's rhetoric back to the character's self-dramatizing impulse. The self-dramatizing impulse itself, as it appears more frequently in the Elizabethan age, will be the subject of numerous essays in the twenties. But the 1919 essay shows what a careful—and original—reader of Shakespeare Eliot already is.

Two other points Eliot will make much of later are raised in this early period. In the essay on Kipling already referred to, when Eliot speaks of Kipling's use of ideas, he comments that "some poets, like Shakespeare or Dante or Villon, and some novelists, like Mr. Conrad, have, in contrast to ideas or concepts, points of view, or 'worlds'—what are incorrectly called 'philosophies.'" And after some detailed remarks on Conrad: "Mr. Conrad has no ideas, but he has a point of view, a 'World'; it can hardly be defined, but it pervades his work and is unmistakable."[15] In discussions throughout the twenties Eliot will worry and elaborate on this notion of something that is seemingly intellectual in Shakespeare and others, yet that is not a "philosophy" or a set of "ideas."

Finally, the issue of development in Shakespeare from the beginning to the end of his career is raised at this time. Eliot will revert to it a good deal toward 1930 and then make it the main theme of his 1937 Shakespeare Lectures. In the *Egoist* "Reflections on Contemporary Poetry" already mentioned Eliot decries the randomness and incoherence of "experiments" among contemporary poets, and he offers Shakespeare as a standard: "We can object that almost none of the experimenters [now] hold fast to anything permanent under varied phenomena of experiment. Shakespeare was one of the slowest, if one of the most persistent, of experimenters." Eliot goes on to speak of the need for a poet's work to show "process."[16] In the "Blake" essay of 1920 we are told that Blake's early poems show "immense power of assimilation," that at this stage "he is very eighteenth century"; then Eliot explains how concentration upon certain ideas leads Blake to the powerful results of the next stage of poems. Eliot says by the way, "Blake's beginnings as a poet, then, are as normal as the beginnings of Shakespeare"; we have already been told that the "peculiar honesty" that characterizes Blake's mature work is a quality shared with Shakespeare. Clearly, the implication is that Shakespeare should be seen as working through the same natural "phases" of development Blake is shown to have worked through.[17] Eliot hints at a view of Shakespeare's progress in answer to a spirited nineteenth-century tradition of theorizing on this matter, from Coleridge through Dowden even to A. C. Bradley.[18] Eliot needs to say more about the details of his view, but already in these early years he clearly accepts the fact of a serious progress in Shakespeare, as he does the greatness and power of Shakespeare, his perfection as an artist, the interest of his language, and other points to be developed in subsequent criticism.

The "Hamlet" Essay

"Hamlet and His Problems," originally a September 1919 *Athenaeum* review of J. M. Robertson's *The Problem of "Hamlet,"* is Eliot's first attempt to speak about Shakespeare in an extended way. Of course, the essay aroused controversy, as Robertson's own work was beginning to do in these years; the controversy is documented by William Quillian in *"Hamlet" and the New Poetic.* And critics have continued to discuss the meaning of Eliot's proposal of "objective correlative" as a counter idea to the sort of confusion or unsatisfactoriness he found in *Hamlet.*[19]

Here I will make some observations on Eliot's intentions in the essay, bringing into consideration his remarks on Shakespeare and related subjects he considers in other essays of this same time. I also discuss the use Eliot makes in the essay of other critics—Robertson, Stoll, A. C. Bradley, and, I suggest, George Pierce Baker, who was one of Eliot's teachers at Harvard. My argument is that Eliot means, in being somewhat outrageous about *Hamlet,* to offer a new standard for the Shakespeare play, something along the lines of the successful "play as a whole" that is "uninterpretable." Eliot wishes to direct our enthusiasm away from *Hamlet* toward the relatively nelected later work, *Antony and Cleopatra* and *Coriolanus.* The proposal of "objective correlative" is one means to Eliot's positive end with the essay, a redirecting of our attention within the Shakespeare canon.

In the first sentence of the essay Eliot says we must admit that "the play" is the problem, and not Hamlet the character. And he goes on to castigate nineteenth-century critics who were tempted to speculate on the character alone and to impose their own personalities on him. He says of Goethe and Coleridge, "probably neither of these men in writing about Hamlet remembered that his first business was to study a work of art."[20] In his second paragraph (added to the original essay for *The Sacred Wood* reprinting) Eliot praises E. E. Stoll's recent pamphlet on the play for calling attention to seventeenth- and eighteenth-century critics; Eliot quotes Stoll declaring that these critics were "nearer in spirit to Shakespeare's art" and "nearer . . . to the secret of dramatic art in general," because "they insisted on the importance of the effect of the whole rather than on the importance of the leading character" (*SE,* pp. 121–22). "Hamlet the play," "a work of art," "the effect of the whole"—this idea of the play as a whole is the artistic criterion that Eliot seeks to promote in his essay. He would like us to think about *Hamlet* differently than we have done. He would like us to see it, as he says a couple of pages on, as an *"artistic* failure" (my emphasis), that is, a failure by a certain criterion.

To accept this criterion is to be able to open ourselves to the later tragedies, especially *Coriolanus* and *Antony*. The idea of "objective correlative" will be offered to direct our interest the same way. Eliot does not deny that Hamlet the character holds great interest or that the play itself is ultimately great. He is clear about the distinction he wants to make in a *Dial* "London Letter" of 1922 that refers to the "Hamlet" essay and to the controversy it caused: "The issue . . . is *not* whether other plays of Shakespeare are 'greater' or 'better' than *Hamlet,* but whether that play is a perfect artistic whole."[21] *Hamlet* may be great for a number of reasons; Eliot would like us to think about what a "perfect artistic whole" is and to consider which of Shakespeare's works best answer to this idea.

The idea of the play as a whole is one Eliot may have been sparked into thinking about by his Harvard teacher George Pierce Baker (who conducted a theater workshop attended by Eugene O'Neill, Thomas Wolfe, and other famous students, and who eventually moved to Yale and founded the Yale Drama School). In 1909–10 Eliot took Baker's course on English drama from the Middle Ages to 1640;[22] later, Eliot recommended Baker's book on Shakespeare for his extension lectures in England in 1918–19.[23] Baker's *The Development of Shakespeare as a Dramatist* (1907) begins with an account of Elizabethan drama in general—the stage conditions, the types of plays—and then moves through Shakespeare's career, discussing various plays in detail.[24] Throughout the book Baker stresses that the interest of all this drama is plot or "story in action" more than it is characterization. Shakespeare may gain great interest by his characterization or intimation of "laws of human conduct," "great laws and forces." But the successful plays bring everything into a whole through mastery of "emphasis" and "proportion," a whole of enacted story that keeps the audience's interest and gets an important emotional response.[25] In certain remarks on Shakespeare's earliest successes (as he sees them) Baker sounds remarkably like Eliot on dramatic form in the "Ben Jonson" and "Massinger" essays: the lack of characterization in *Titus Andronicus* suits the "melodramatic" purpose of that play (Baker, pp. 123–34), and the specific amount of characterization in *Comedy of Errors* suits the purpose of "farce-comedy" (pp. 134–41). Baker does not set out to criticize *Hamlet;* indeed, he makes a point to defend the fourth act as being good on the story level (pp. 264–74). He sees in the later work, notably in *Coriolanus,* a falling off and loss of control (pp. 286–91).

Whatever Eliot may owe to Baker, he developed his own view of the play as a whole, centered in action, a developed view to which the opening paragraphs of the "Hamlet" essay point. In "Ben Jonson" (originally two essays, 1919) Eliot calls attention to "the design of the whole." He goes to great trouble to define the special nature of Jonson's "creative satire," where the scale of the characters and the way of outlining them suit the overall purpose and form. What is important is the *"total effect"* (Eliot's emphasis). "Volpone's life . . . is bounded by the scene in which it is played; in fact, the life is the life of the scene and is derivatively the life of Volpone; the life of the character is inseparable from the life of the drama." A "unity of inspiration" holds everything together, forming plot and characters both. The Jonson play is a "world," interesting not because of the subject matter, but because the subject matter "leads to an authentic result . . . projects a new world into a new orbit."[26] (Throughout this discussion there are contrasts drawn with Shakespeare, which I shall come back to in discussing character creation in the next chapter; these contrasts do not gainsay the idea of unity, and centeredness in action, as a standard for Shakespeare's drama as well as Jonson's.)

In "Philip Massinger" (also originally two essays, 1920) Eliot reproaches Fletcher and Massinger for trying "to put together heterogeneous parts" to form plays; he speaks of the greater dramatists' "ability to perform that slight distortion of *all* the elements in the world of a play or a story, so that the world is complete in itself. . . ."[27] Eliot offers here a view of unity in drama in the tradition of Coleridge, who spoke of Shakespeare's working "in the spirit of nature," "from within by evolution and assimilation," in contrast to other dramatists who stuck together really unbelonging parts to give the illusion of a whole; though Coleridge wished to distinguish Shakespeare from *all* his contemporaries.[28] Eliot's general disposition toward wholeness at this time, to want to understand the part by reference to the whole, is also seen in his 1919 essay on Donne's sermons, where it is said we must read whole sermons in order to understand the emphasis of any part. Indeed, the sermon is compared to the drama as being "applied" art, where the conveying of a "structure" to the audience is the paramount thing (the details, it is implied, amount to the "application" of the structure).[29] In the 1920 "Dante" essay Eliot's central point is that every episode or emotion must be taken in the context of the whole.[30] (Here, as with Ben Jonson, a contrast is drawn with Shakespeare, who analyzes and dissolves where Dante orders and places; but the contrast is not one that contradicts the general idea of wholeness as a standard for Shakespeare—the work must be seen through to the end [*SW*, p. 168].)

In the "Hamlet" essay, once Eliot has raised the idea of the play as a whole, he brings up Robertson's points about the gradual development of *Hamlet* in various versions as a way of accounting for the play's inconsistencies. But Eliot begins this discussion with a statement which can seem cryptic: "*Qua* work of art, the work of art cannot be interpreted; there is nothing to interpret." Then he says the only conceivable sense for "interpretation" is to consider such historical facts as Robertson points out (*SE*, p. 122).

This idea of the work of art as presenting nothing to be thought about or gotten behind, as presenting to us directly all that it has to present, is an important qualification to the concept of the play as a whole. The idea of the work as not properly interpretable is one Eliot will develop with special regard to poetic drama in a series of essays going well into the twenties (I discuss this thinking in the next chapter). But already, by the time of the "Hamlet" essay, Eliot has shown a considerable disposition against interpreting or *thinking about* the work of art—with the implication that the preferred art does not ask such a reaction (as *Hamlet* seems to do). We have seen that Eliot is ready, with J. B. Yeats, to chide the naming and categorizing sort of mind that might be seen as Bunyanesque with regard to the work of Shakespeare. We have seen other instances of objection to the taming or making comfortable of Shakespeare, in effect the translating of him into new terms, on the part of critics. In the "Duchess of Malfi" piece Eliot objects to actors' "making" of parts, doing an invalid sort of interpretation, rather than transmitting the dramatic poetry directly. He makes a similar objection to actors' interpretations in "Four Elizabethan Dramatists" (1924).[31] In general, Eliot craves a direct confrontation with the work of art, an open "enjoyment." At the beginning of the article on Kipling he says we are not curious or brave enough to examine Kipling.[32] In "Beyle and Balzac" he says the literary historian needs primarily to enjoy all and to beware of "shaping" his material with an idea.[33] In "Ben Jonson" the theory of humors is said to obscure the plays. For a new look at Dryden, "delight" is all the point.[34]

From the time of Eliot's earliest work he favors a sort of open acceptance in regard to life—this is a general state of mind he would like to see prevail. In a 1916 review of A. J. Balfour's *Theism and Humanism* he pleads for acceptance of the world and feeling as opposed to "belief about"; in both "theism" and "naturalism" there is a remove from life into thought.[35] In 1917 he complains of Wundt's *Elements of Folk Psychology* that there is too much of *a priori* categories, an imposed philosophy of history, too much "external" brought to the material.[36] And Eliot objects that Collingwood's *Religion and Philosophy* generalizes religion too much, neglects the historical particulars in which it appears.[37] Good philosophy and good tragedy are considered "statements," presentations of a mood, as opposed to "talking about."[38] In the dialogue "Eeldrop and Appleplex" (Eliot and Pound?) the two characters set out to escape "the pigeon-holed," to seek out "concrete individuality" in their observations of life and their discussions.[39] Elizabethan prose writers are praised for their open-eyedness as opposed to the "idealization" of writers on the First World War.[40] Eliot complains of "moral cowardice" in the English literary world, a shying away from any point of view which cannot be sorted under a known religious or political title.[41]

The great virtue for the artist himself is just this acceptance of life and his material. Henry James is praised for his mastery of and escape from ideas[42] (indeed, William James is praised for resistance to the "oppressiveness" of familiar philosophical ideas);[43] while Henry Adams is faulted for his inability to be "interested," to be "passionately absorbed."[44] With regard to Blake (who escaped the malady) it is noted that ideas obscure what we are and feel.[45] The modern "psychoanalytic" novel is criticized for its too clearly defined material, defined as it were in advance;[46] while part of the praise of *Ulysses* is that the artist's material is "accepted."[47] Donne is praised for his fidelity to the emotion as he finds it and his refusal to avoid complexity of feeling, alterations, and antitheses.[48] With regard to Elizabethan drama the "Massinger" essay states that the creator of character needs not knowledge of motives, or "understanding," but "keen sensibility," "exceptional awareness" of people (*SE*, p. 188). He must just *see*. It is difficult to think of the author of *Hamlet* as not accepting his material and producing the suitable complex result in art. But Eliot seems to have in mind an art where the artist is open to life but transcribes it so *clearly* and with such perfect techniques of art that the attitude of openness can be carried on from artist to audience without the need for "thinking" at any point.

Eliot makes use of Robertson's discussion of the versions of *Hamlet* to illuminate his own critical point about this play and other Shakespeare plays, which he comes to in the heart of the essay. Eliot engages certain other traditions and trends of Shakespeare criticism as well, all for the purpose of elaborating his own distinct view. But before we come to this view, we must be clear about these traditions and where Eliot stands in regard to them.

As the beginning of the essay notes, the tradition of speculating about Hamlet's character as a primary entry into the play belongs to the late eighteenth and nineteenth centuries. This approach culminates in A. C. Bradley (before the waves of post-World War II Freudian readings), who sums up earlier views and proposes his own idea of "melancholy" as a recently developed malaise in the character, accounting for the fact that so much of Hamlet's behavior seems to go against his real and deeper traits.[49] Eliot recommends Bradley's *Four Tragedies of Shakespeare* (*sic*) in the syllabus for his Elizabethan extension course, calling the book "an excellent study."[50] But at the end of the essay "Swinburne as Critic" Eliot questions whether Bradley is one of those critics "interested in extracting something from their subject which is not fairly in it." In a "London Letter" of 1922 he calls *Four Tragedies* a "needless luxury" and ranks Bradley with those gentlemanly critics who lack "punch."[51]

Whatever Bradley may have meant to Eliot, the work of Stoll, Robertson, Schücking, and other scholars in the first two decades of the century came as a reaction against Bradley and the nineteenth-century critics behind him, whom Eliot does name in the "Hamlet" essay. These new scholars sought to direct attention to Elizabethan conventions of the stage, general morality, and the understanding of human nature and to reinterpret the plays as they were likely to have been taken by their original audiences. Stoll, for example, looking at the Vice tradition, spoke against the sentimentalization of Shylock, Falstaff, and other characters and stressed the artificiality all this drama was likely to have had for its entertainment-craving audiences (a point very close to Schücking).[52]

Related to this new scholarship and interpretation was the increasing amount of stage production of Shakespeare in Elizabethan style—without nineteenth-century scenic encumbrances and with complete and unaltered texts. Already William Poel had produced plays in the late nineteenth century; Granville-Barker's productions began soon after the turn of the century.[53] Eliot took a great interest from 1919 on in productions of Shakespeare and others (including Restoration dramatists) in correct style by the Phoenix Society, a diverse and changing group. Eliot was interested even if he considered the production unsuccessful, as he did *The Duchess of Malfi* in 1919; he gave great praise to later productions of *Volpone* and *King Lear*.[54]

Eliot praises Stoll and Robertson in the "Hamlet" essay, and he thought historical scholarship important enough that he fostered it for many years in *The Criterion*—though he admits contradictory views there, notable Dover Wilson's vigorous attacks on Robertson's textual studies (see the appendix, where I list and describe *The Criterion* scholarly articles on Shakespeare and Elizabethan drama). But it is important to realize that Eliot does not align himself with the views of Stoll or Robertson or any one of the new scholars. He makes use of *certain points* for his own purposes. Stoll has no intention to criticize *Hamlet* or to foster interest in neglected plays of Shakespeare where something like "objective correlative" may be seen to account for the aesthetic achievement. He insists that Hamlet the character is a "romantic hero" with no curious psychological problems; that his soliloquies and other divagations are just a part of Shakespeare's skillful handling of the action, to keep revenge before us without bringing it off; and that the play centers in "intrigue, fate, and blood"—a successful theater piece for a "simple and healthy . . . romantic" audience.[55] Stoll's idea of the Elizabethan play is one of thrilling, not especially thought-provoking, action for a rather simple multitude; he sees *Hamlet* as fulfilling this idea very well.

Robertson, of course, sees plenty of imperfection in the play, and he accounts for it with his theory of the stages of composition, in work previous to Shakespeare and in Shakespeare, which Eliot rehearses in the essay. Robertson differs from Stoll further in that he sees Shakespeare's Hamlet as indeed a depressed and unstable character, dominated by Shakespeare's newly introduced motive of obsession with the mother. But Robertson is like Stoll in finding the play ultimately a success, though in different terms. Despite all the incompatible material left over from earlier versions of the play, Shakespeare has brought off a "triumph" in impressing on us the nature of his newly conceived protagonist:

> Shakespeare's handling of the play is above all things a masterly effort to hint a psychological solution of the acted mystery [the delay], while actually heightening it by the self-accusing soliloquies.
>
> . . . the play becomes only more wonderful when the manner of its evolution is realized . . . What [Shakespeare] did remains a miracle of dramatic imagination . . . he has

projected a personality which from the first line sets all our sympathies in a quick vibration, and . . . holds our minds and hearts.[56]

In sum, Stoll's general idea of the Elizabethan play is one Eliot at least wishes to modify; he wants to propose an ideal that *Hamlet* does not measure up to. And Robertson's "disintegration" of the text, for a work he finally admires as a "triumph" and a "miracle," is for Eliot just a tool to help explain his own *critical* dissatisfaction with the play and desire to investigate other works by Shakespeare.[57]

Eliot rehearses Robertson's account of the various versions of *Hamlet* in story and drama. He sums up by saying that Shakespeare wished to show us the effect of a mother's guilt upon her son, but that he could not "impose" this motive upon the "intractable" material that came down to him (*SE,* p. 123). Eliot dwells on the "intractability" and speculates on further problems Shakespeare had with the play, which Robertson did not suggest. Eliot accepts Robertson's point about "superfluous and inconsistent scenes" in the play; he is bothered, moreover, by "variableness" in the versification, citing "Look, the morn, in russet mantle clad . . ." against Hamlet's pithy account later of his doings at night aboard ship on the journey.

Distinctly beyond Robertson, Eliot sees difficulties on Shakespeare's part not only with the theme of the mother, but also with subjects that cannot even be specified. There is much that cannot be "handled." Eliot is dissatisfied in that he perceives something in the play "not in the action, not in any quotations that we might select, so much as in an unmistakable tone" (p. 124). "Tone" is not defined; nor is it made clear why tone, if present, is insufficient art. But is something really there? Hamlet's emotion is "in excess" of the facts that appear. The emotion is not really there, though we have some sense of it; it is "inexpressible" (p. 125). And Hamlet's "madness" just shows the defeat of Shakespeare with an emotion he cannot bring to light in art (pp. 125–26). Eliot's points against *Hamlet* do not go very far. What they suggest is in Eliot himself something like a *taste* against the play, particularly in a matter such as the "variableness" of the versification. It is notable that Eliot overcomes his distaste, later praising the careful changes in style of verse throughout the first scene as constituting a "musical pattern," and speaking of the play altogether as being a great success, the decisive achievement of Shakespeare's middle career, justified in its great popularity in all ages.[58]

Eliot expresses somewhat incompletely a distaste for *Hamlet;* more important, he gives us a positive standard at every turn. After speaking of the "superfluous and inconsistent scenes" and "variableness" of the versification in *Hamlet,* he says we must place the play in a "period of crisis" along with *Measure for Measure,* which is also "profoundly interesting," and has "astonishing versification." Then follow the "tragic successes" leading up to *Coriolanus:* "*Coriolanus* may not be as 'interesting' as *Hamlet,* but it is, with *Antony and*

Cleopatra, Shakespeare's most assured artistic success" (p. 124). There is the virtual admission here that *Hamlet* is "profoundly interesting" and that its versification is "astonishing," however "variable." It is notable that for the 1918– 19 extension course the Shakespeare reading, after an early comedy, is *Measure for Measure,* as if that play without *Hamlet's* fame, or the tradition of bad habits in thinking about it, might better represent the mature Shakespeare, the Shakespeare of the "period of crisis"; then, for "the later Shakespeare," "Read: *Coriolanus,* or the *Winter's Tale,* or *Antony and Cleopatra.*"[59] The criticism of *Hamlet* and invocation of a "period of crisis" in Shakespeare bring Eliot to recommend the string of "tragic successes," especially *Coriolanus* and *Antony,* together "Shakespeare's most assured artistic success." *Artistic* success—we are bound to think at this point of the idea of the play as a whole, where character and action and, presumably, a fully articulated atmosphere work as one; nothing is "superfluous" or "inconsistent," and there is no "variableness" in the verse—everything is telling, and all works on one consistently maintained plane. One thinks too of the idea of the work of art that is not to be interpreted, that presents directly all that it has to present.

It is something of a shock to be asked to turn our attention away from *Hamlet* and toward the later tragedies, *Coriolanus* above all. That play had never roused much interest. Bradley discussed it in his 1912 British Academy lecture as a decidedly limited work: "Shakespeare closed the door on certain effects, in the absence of which his whole power in tragedy could not be displayed."[60] G. P. Baker calls *Coriolanus* a failure outright, indicating a loss of control of story details on Shakespeare's part and having an uninteresting main character.[61] Eliot's comments make us start to ask—some hints having been given toward an answer—what in fact is an "artistic success" in drama? Is there something in the later tragedies, *Coriolanus* above all, that has been missed?

Just below this point Eliot outlines more of what it is he wants. Where he suggests that Shakespeare in *Hamlet* struggled with material of his own beyond the guilt of a mother, he notes: "It is not merely the 'guilt of a mother' that cannot be handled as Shakespeare handled the suspicion of Othello, the infatuation of Antony, or the pride of Coriolanus. The subject might conceivably have expanded into a tragedy like these, intelligible, self-complete, in the sunlight." Eliot goes on to say he does not find Shakespeare's Hamlet in the speeches or action but in an "unmistakable tone" (p. 124). The noted successes of Shakespeare are "self-complete"; that is, they function as wholes, everything being necessary, and all that is necessary being given. And these plays are "intelligible"; whatever motivates them is fully realized in the lines and action— there is no requirement of, no invitation to, "interpretation." There are discernible subjects—suspicion, infatuation, pride—but these subjects are made thoroughly into plays where the main character is not more intriguing than the action as a whole.

Next, in a paragraph about Hamlet's emotion being in excess of the facts as they appear, comes the suggestion about "objective correlatives," the way to express emotion in art. One wants "a set of objects, a situation, a chain of events which shall be the formula of that *particular* emotion; such that when the external facts, which must terminate in sensory experience, are given, the emotion is immediately evoked." In Shakespeare's "successful" tragedies we will find this "exact equivalence":

> you will find that the state of mind of Lady Macbeth walking in her sleep has been communicated to you by a skillful accumulation of imagined sensory impressions; the words of Macbeth on hearing of his wife's death strike us as if, given the sequence of events, these words were automatically released by the last event in the series. The artistic "inevitability" lies in this complete adequacy of the external to the emotion. [pp. 124–25]

The "set of objects" is a remarkably open conception, like the phrase "objective correlative" itself. This openness probably accounts for the perdurable interest of this passage. We are bound to say Eliot is thinking about imagery in the widest sense of the term: "external facts" equate to "a set of objects, a situation, a chain of events," and the "external facts" are said to "terminate in sensory experience." The example of the Lady Macbeth scene leaves no doubt about this. (Eliot often wishes to talk about imagery in a wider sense than the purely visual. He writes of Pound's Cantos in 1928 that the poet's eye is "careful, comprehensive, and exact"; "but it is rare that he has an image of the maximum concentration, an image which combines the precise and concrete with a kind of almost infinite suggestion.")[62]

At the same time, Eliot is talking about the giving of information or the making clear of the action *in its own terms*. Macbeth's words are acceptable to us—indeed they seem inevitable—as an event in a precisely ordered series. But the plausibility—or inevitability—of the series comes not because Shakespeare has given us in Macbeth a simply understood, simply motivated character, or because he has made clear to us that blank depression is the natural response to the death of a spouse. Macbeth's words take their place in a pattern of divagations of mood, including fear, anger, and depression, a pattern that has been made familiar to us as the way of Macbeth, especially in the latter portion of the play.

Let us look more closely at this example from *Macbeth*. When Macbeth hears of his wife's death, he at first goes rather blank: "She should have died hereafter; / There would have been a time for such a word." Then, after a pause (I would say), he sinks deeply, abstracted, making the extended reflection, "Tomorrow, and tomorrow, and tomorrow." The reflection is succeeded by a recall to events and a quite engaged, if bitter, reaction to them: "(*Enter a Messenger*) Thou com'st to use thy tongue; thy story quickly!" (V, v, 17–29). This sequence accords with fluctuations we are used to in Macbeth's behavior. In the scenes immediately preceding this speech he has wavered rapidly among bravado; anger for no immediate reason, suggesting a deeper frustration; abstracted, depressed reflection; indirect confession of distress (as with the Doctor).

Parallel to the reaction to Lady Macbeth's death, Macbeth has reacted to the announcement of the English force of ten thousand with a sudden plunge into depressed reflection:

> This push
> Will cheer me ever, or disseat me now.
> I have lived long enough. My way of life
> Is fall'n into the sear, the yellow leaf. . . .

And as with the reflection upon Lady Macbeth's death, at the end there is a sudden recall to present events:

> . . . mouth-honour, breath,
> Which the poor heart would fain deny, and dare not.
> Seyton! (*Enter Seyton*) [V, iii, 20–29]

The sequence of thoughts upon Lady Macbeth's death is in one aspect familiar to us and comes the more "inevitably." We see Macbeth moving through shock, abstraction, and arousal to events in a way the play has established as a procedure for him. The depressed thoughts are not so much thought as such (*Bedeutung*) as they are Macbeth-like. The speech is "sensory experience" for us of a sort, taking its place in a consistent plane of dramatic realization. The play is entirely present to us—if we will look—not asking interpretation.

There is no absolute formulation for "objective correlative" or for the idea of the uninterpretable play as a whole. Eliot's writing forces us (and it is his intention, I maintain) to look at *Coriolanus, Antony,* and the other later plays with a renewed interest and with a new idea in mind of what a thoroughly "successful" play might be, a non-absolute idea ready to be specified with regard to the individual work. This concept accords with the look back at the "Hamlet" essay Eliot takes in "To Criticize the Critic":

Now what of the generalizations, and the phrases which have flourished, such as "dissociation of sensibility" and "objective correlative"? . . . they have served their turn as stimuli to the critical thinking of others . . . these phrases may be accounted for as being conceptual symbols for emotional preferences . . . The "objective correlative" in the essay on Hamlet may stand for my bias towards the more mature plays of Shakespeare—*Timon, Antony and Cleopatra, Coriolanus* notably . . . these concepts, these generalizations, had their origin in my sensibility. They arise from my feeling of kinship with one poet or with one kind of poetry rather than another . . . my own theorizing has been epiphenomenal of my tastes.[63]

Eliot is not saying that his concepts are negligible; rather, his purpose with them is to bring us into sympathy with his sensibility for particular works— *Timon, Antony,* and so on.

Finally, when Eliot speaks of Hamlet's "madness" as "the buffoonery of an emotion which [the dramatist] cannot express in art," he goes on to make a general comment on what the artist does with "the intense feeling, ecstatic or terrible, without an object or exceeding its object . . . which every person of sensibility has known": "The artist keeps [such feelings] alive by his ability to intensify the world to his emotions" (*SE*, p. 126). *Hamlet* provokes us to do too much speculating; it does not amount to the thorough "intensification" into a world of art—action, sensory experience—of the originating feeling, what Shakespeare shows to be the way of art in his "more successful tragedies." Eliot concludes the whole "Hamlet" essay in its original appearance in the *Athenaeum* with a comment he omitted from *The Sacred Wood* and later reprintings: "In The Storm in 'Lear,' and in the last scene of 'Othello,' Shakespeare triumphed in tearing art from the impossible."[64] Eliot probably omitted this comment because he thought more needed to be said. But it is clear he has in mind with these scenes the bringing of the artist's originating feeling—profound, "impossible"—to fully realized art—a thorough "intensification," "a set of objects, a situation, a chain of events," "terminating in sensory experience." With the storm in *Lear* particularly we are aware of the consistency of character, action, and articulated atmosphere, all as one, that has been suggested in the "objective correlative" passage.

One leaves the "Hamlet" essay wondering whether *Hamlet* might be defended in terms Eliot would admit or wondering in what other terms the play might be defended. This is surely healthy speculation. But more important with regard to the scope of Eliot's Shakespeare criticism, one leaves the essay with a new general idea of the fully achieved work of art and a new interest in plays of Shakespeare besides *Hamlet*—well-accepted ones like *Macbeth* and relatively neglected ones like *Coriolanus*. What Eliot has positively to suggest in this essay fits with the view he is developing of Shakespeare and of poetic drama in general, in a range of places in the work of the early 1920s.

2

The 1920s: Developing a View of the Shakespeare Play

Eliot wrote the "Hamlet" essay at a time when he was making a number of references to Shakespeare attesting to his greatness as an artist, the interest of his language, and other points. These relatively brief discussions show that Eliot had a varied and serious interest in Shakespeare in these early years, though no thought-out view of Shakespeare's drama is yet explained. Nevertheless, the small discussions accord with later explanations and may indicate radical early insights that Eliot felt bound to pursue later. The "Hamlet" essay is certainly meant to make positive suggestions about the successful Shakespeare play—something along the lines of the "uninterpretable play-as-a-whole." But the endless discussability of this essay, the perennial controversy, is evidence that Eliot does not make himself clear here. He needs to say more about his idea of the Shakespeare play.

In the years between 1919 and the next extended discussion of Shakespeare in 1927, "Shakespeare and the Stoicism of Seneca," Eliot does elaborate a view of Shakespearean drama in a range of places. He discusses Shakespeare's use of language, the created character, and the whole "poetic vision" that is to be conveyed to the audience. And at every stage Eliot is concerned with the reaction of the audience—how it is made to be involved in the work.

Another strain in Eliot's comments on Shakespeare in this period is a growing dissatisfaction with the Elizabethan age—its state of mind, its artistic forms—from which Shakespeare is not quite to be exempted. At least the issue of Shakespeare's exemption worries Eliot; he is not to resolve it until the years around 1930, when he thinks harder about the question of meaning or substantive vision in Shakespeare. Even in times of doubt, however, it is notable that *The Criterion* steadily publishes other writers than Eliot taking the highest view of Shakespeare and the most unreserved philosophical interest in him (see the appendix).

Language

The points about Shakespeare's language Eliot makes repeatedly in the twenties may be grouped under three headings: the closeness of word to object, the nature of Shakespeare's metaphor as realization of thought, and the perfection of the language. The perfection of the language is partly a matter of being fully achieved, of Shakespeare's mastery as an artist, and partly a matter of his making the most of an historical opportunity, taking the language where historical circumstances enabled it to go.

In "Swinburne as Poet" (1920), which is in the main a defense of Swinburne's "diffuseness" as being his special quality, Eliot says of him that it is the word, not the object, that matters in his verse. When his verse is analyzed, the object is not there.

> Compare
>
> Snowdrops that plead for pardon
> And pine for fright
>
> with the daffodils that come before the swallow dares. The snowdrop of Swinburne disappears, the daffodil of Shakespeare remains. The swallow of Shakespeare remains in the verse in *Macbeth*. [*SE*, p. 284]

By invoking the Shakespearean standard for the poet's getting the "thrill" from the object, having the object "remain" in his verse, Eliot is not setting up an idea of "reality" as something knowable apart from words, something from which words may stray to a greater or lesser degree. Nor is he saying that Shakespeare is "more referential" than Swinburne. The point is that Shakespearean poetry gives us the sense of an object—it conceivably creates the sense, or the object, and the object "remains in the verse." Eliot's concern with word and object is a wide one in the early essays; he pursues the question with poetry of all periods. I shall not take space to explain this whole interest. But note that though Eliot is concerned about the poet's being realistic, or true to observable reality, the final emphasis of his criticism is the same one that appears in this remark on Shakespeare and Swinburne: the isolation of a kind of poetry that gives the *sense* of an object, a poetry where the object inheres, "remains in the verse."[1]

The "Blake" essay, by implication, attributes closeness of word and object to Shakespeare under the notion of "honesty." The essay calls Blake's quality "a peculiar honesty," and this is said to be found in Shakespeare, as well as in Homer, Dante, and other poets (*SE*, p. 275). Eliot is speaking of a moral quality, of course, but the essay makes clear that there is no line to be drawn between the moral insight and the verse with its sense of the object ("this honesty never exists without great technical accomplishment" [p. 275]). As mentioned before, Eliot associates Blake with Shakespeare in development from the conventional to something amazing and new. Eliot describes the mature Blake as having "interest" in and "knowledge" of human emotions: "The emotions are presented in an extremely simplified, abstract form . . . Blake . . . knew what interested him, and he therefore presents only the essential, only, in fact, what can be presented, and need not be explained" (p. 277). Here the notion of the object is extended to "emotions"; the triumph is still a matter of "presentation," of having the object or emotion there in the verse. Blake's later, long poems are seen to fail not because they are visionary or remote from the world, but because "Blake did not see enough, became too much occupied with ideas" (pp. 278–79). Eliot denies that he would have as a criterion the weighing the poems against the familiar, observable world. The point, again, is that the poetry needs to give us something to "see," however daring. The argument about Blake—Shakespeare is also involved in the argument—is that one kind of great poetry works by keeping before us something, even an emotion, "to be seen."

In the "Massinger" essay, still in 1920, Eliot is explicit about Shakespeare once again. After giving two pages of pairs of passages from Massinger and Shakespeare, Eliot concludes that Massinger's "feeling for language" goes beyond his "feeling for things." His eye and his words are not at one. With the end of the Jacobean generation, which includes Donne and some of the later playwrights, "we end a period when the intellect was immediately at the tips of the senses. Sensation became word and word was sensation" (*SE,* p. 185). This comment recalls the earlier essay on Swinburne's criticism with its remark on "thinking through the senses," about which Eliot feels more needs to be said; now Eliot offers to say that "more." In Shakespeare we are not so much referred to reality as put in a new area that is hard to describe—"sensation became word and word was sensation." The *effect* is one of "feeling for things" in good proportion to "feeling for language," of eye and vocabulary "in co-operation." Language in some sense evokes the object, or, as with Blake, "emotion," or simply "feeling" that is not just "feeling for language." "Every vital development in language is a development of feeling as well. The verse of Shakespeare and the major Shakespearean dramatists is an innovation of this kind . . . The verse practiced by Massinger seems to lead us away from feeling altogether" (pp. 185–86). Eliot comments on a speech of Massinger with involved syntax as suffering from "cerebral anaemia." "Such a style should follow the involutions of a mode of perceiving, registering, and digesting impressions which is also involved" (p. 187). The verse of Shakespeare, Donne, and some of the later dramatists suggests a "mode of perceiving." Again, note that Eliot does not declare that this verse refers to an already established "mode of perceiving"; the mode may be there for the first time. Instead, this verse suggests a mode we *take* to be one of "perceiving, registering, and digesting."

The subject of metaphor is not to be separated from that of word and object. As Eliot noted in "Studies in Contemporary Criticism" (1918), which quotes the "strong toil of grace" line, with such a figure one cannot say where the literal and metaphorical meet. The burden of Eliot's comment on Shakespeare's metaphor during the twenties is that the metaphor is the realization of thought. Thought is, as it were, the object. The metaphor, like the word, presents us with something we want to call real, not just "feeling for language." The senses are involved; as Eliot put it in the 1918 essay, the metaphor makes use of physical energy. Eliot is quite explicit that metaphor presents us with what we do not quite already know, what is not to be known except in the poet's language—just as the word gives us not the object we already know, but what we accept newly as being an object.

The "Massinger" essay is the important starting point for this line of thinking. The pairs of passages from Massinger and Shakespeare all serve to illustrate Shakespeare's vividness, particularity, and his appeal to the senses—one image, it is said, "appears to the eye and makes us catch our breath" (*SE,* p. 184). If we look at a pair of passages where each is one extended metaphor, we can see all the points involved in Eliot's thinking.

> MASSINGER: Thou didst not borrow of Vice her indirect,
>   Crooked, and abject means.
> SHAKESPEARE: God knows, my son;
>   By what by-paths and indirect crook'd ways
>   I met this crown.
>
> . . . Massinger gives the general forensic statement, Shakespeare the particular image. "Indirect crook'd" is forceful in Shakespeare; a mere pleonasm in Massinger. "Crook'd ways" is a metaphor; Massinger's phrase only the ghost of a metaphor. [p. 183]

"'Indirect crook'd' is forceful in Shakespeare; a mere pleonasm in Massinger." That is, the words in Massinger are more than is necessary, a rhetorical translation of something that might be known by just one word instead of two, or conceivably by another word than either of these. "Forceful" must mean "necessary"; the words said, in their entirety, convey what is meant. For a moment we wander with Henry on those "by-paths and indirect crook'd ways" and thus *know* how he came to the crown. "'Crook'd ways' is a metaphor; Massinger's phrase only the ghost of a metaphor." Massinger uses a figure of ways or roads, with "indirect" and "crooked" applied to a figure of Vice with her "means"; this double distancing gives the sense of conventional, not freshly considered, figurative language—Massinger's statement is "forensic." There is the implication that the point might have been made another way. The *real* metaphor, as opposed to the "ghost," must be the statement that has to be said as it is, the new thing finding its perfect identity.

Later in the essay Eliot says of the Jacobeans:

> One of the greatest distinctions of several of them is a gift for combining, for fusing into a single phrase, two or more diverse impressions.

. . . in her strong toil of grace

of Shakespeare is such a fusion; the metaphor identifies itself with what suggests it; the re-
sultant is one and is unique. [p. 185]

The metaphor is necessary to "what suggests it"; the two take form in one
another. The metaphor is a new and singular thing, not just a figurative translation for what might be known in another way. Eliot goes on about this
technique: he quotes lines of Tourneur and Middleton and speaks of the "perpetual slight alteration of language" there and of new combinations and new
meanings. The stress is on the statement as something new. And Eliot says the
"perpetual slight alteration of language" "evidences a very high development of
the senses" (p. 185). We return to the point about closeness of word to object.
Figurative language, the realization of thought or meaning, gives a sense as of
an object, doing so as if by an appeal to our physical senses.

Eliot reiterates this thinking in comments on Shakespeare's language
throughout the twenties. In "The Metaphysical Poets" (1921), where he is
speaking of the variety of techniques in this poetry, he cites Donne, "A bracelet
of bright hair about the bone," and comments on the effect due to a contrast
of associations, a "telescoping" of images with associations thus "multiplied."
This procedure is said to be typical of Shakespeare and other dramatists of the
period (*SE,* p. 243). The point here is close to that of the "Massinger" essay.
What in that essay is called "fusion" of "impressions," as with Shakespeare's
"strong toil" and "grace," to produce something new is now discussed as "telescoping." What Donne does with a few words in series in a description, each
word with its own body of associations, and these associations affecting each
other in "multiplication," is much the same as what Shakespeare does with actual metaphor.

Further on in "The Metaphysical Poets" Eliot speaks of the dramatic verse
of the period in general as expressing a "development of sensibility" (beyond
what the prose of the period expresses). Chapman especially is commended for
"a direct sensuous apprehension of thought, or a recreation of thought into feeling, which is exactly what we find in Donne" (*SE,* pp. 245–46). Language,
with its "fusion" or composite effect, is related directly to sensibility; that is,
language is the realization of thought, thought being conceived more widely
than "abstraction." What language in the end presents is "feeling," an "object"
we know with, we are sure, participation of the senses, what "thought" becomes as it is realized in language.

In later essays Eliot returns to metaphor, strictly speaking, and to Shakespeare's "strong toil of grace" passage. In the second essay on Marvell, a 1923
review of one edition of the poems, Eliot tries to make distinctions in seventeenth-century verse:

When Shakespeare says—

> She looks like sleep,
> As she would catch another Antony
> In her strong toil of grace,

it is not a conceit . . . instead of contrast we have fusion: a restoration of language to contact with things.[2]

"She" and "how she looks" are "fused," and there is also "fusion," as already noted, within the as-if clause itself. In the new thing that has become of all these meanings, there is a sense of closeness—indeed "contact"—between "language" and "things." Eliot, though, is saying quite the opposite to the notion that Shakespeare found the "right" words for some thing we already know, or could know, in terms other than Shakespeare's.

In the same essay Eliot gives some similes from Dante and comments, "They have a rational necessity as well as suggestiveness; they are, like the words of Shakespeare above, an *explication* of the meaning."[3] These figures, in Shakespeare and Dante both, have *necessity;* the meaning is not to be supposed as existing apart from its "explication," which the figures are. In the unpublished Clark Lectures of 1926, Eliot's large-scale discussion of seventeenth-century poetry, this same Shakespeare passage is quoted: "She looks like sleep. . . ." It is said not to have the "*rational* necessity" (my emphasis) of Dante, but it is still "necessary," in contrast to much of the language of seventeenth-century poets. We have in the passage "an image absolutely woven into the fabric of the thought."[4] (A new distinction from Dante is maintained in the "Dante" essay of 1929, but still with no loss in the sense of Shakespeare's "necessity": "Whereas the simile of Dante is merely to make you see more clearly . . . the figure of Shakespeare [still speaking of the *Antony* lines] is expansive rather than intensive; its purpose is to *add* to what you see" [*SE,* p. 205]).

Later in the Clark Lectures Eliot compares Shakespeare with Herbert on the issue of "compression," speculating on the effect of Shakespeare, with his "immense compressions of meaning," upon seventeenth-century poetry in general. Eliot calls Herbert Shakespearean and comments on the last two lines of "Prayer" (I): "Church-bels beyond the starres heard, the souls bloud, / The land of spices; something understood." The direct meanings of each element are seen to cancel each other out, and "an exact suggestion is obtained which is not even partially present in any of the images taken alone; an extension, and no vague one, beyond the bounds of thought."[5] Again, metaphor, or poetry made of metaphors, is seen to be a kind of thought, in this case thought going beyond thought—"an exact suggestion . . . an extension, and no vague one." In a BBC talk on "Devotional Poets" presented in 1930 Eliot quotes all of "Prayer" (I) and says that Herbert achieves a "whole"; the last two lines "reflect a glory on what precedes." The effect of Herbert's work is likened to the "strictly useful" similes and metaphors of Shakespeare and Dante, in contrast to other seventeenth-century poetry where the conceit is enjoyed for itself.[6]

Eliot's remarks on the perfection of Shakespeare's language stress both Shakespeare's individual greatness as an artist and his intuition to develop the language of his day as it was natural to develop it. These remarks are, in a sense, just an extension of those about the "necessity" of Shakespeare's metaphor and the suitability of word to object.

In a letter to the *Times Literary Supplement* in 1928 Eliot comments on a speech of Coriolanus (where that character makes himself known to Aufidius in Antium in act 4, scene 5): he claims that printed as prose the speech is inferior to North's Plutarch, though it is great as poetry—"verse . . . is itself a system of *punctuation*," the verse form itself being necessary to what Shakespeare is saying.[7] The following year, in a BBC talk on "The Tudor Translators," Eliot quotes the passage from *Coriolanus,* calling it a "criticism" of North. "Every change made by Shakespeare is not merely the change from prose to verse, but an absolute improvement in force, concision, and ease of syntax. The verse of Shakespeare is more mature than the prose of North."[8] The verse is thus seen to take the prose a step further in its intellectual—we may say—purposes.

Eliot's twelve BBC talks of 1929 and 1930 give a survey of Elizabethan and seventeenth-century prose and poetry, frequently stressing Shakespeare's achievement in pushing forward intellectual frontiers in the "necessary" form of poetry (the seventh to twelfth talks, on poetry, repeat and rework much of the Clark Lectures). The first talk, "The Tudor Translators," calls the sixteenth and seventeenth centuries "the most exciting period of English literature," and Eliot makes clear that he wants to regard this literature as an expression of the historical development of sensibility, both intellectual and perceptual. In this talk he not only instances the passage from *Coriolanus* as an advance in "force, concision, and ease" over North; he also speaks of *Hamlet,* with no derogatory implications, as a "representation" of "emotional and intellectual crisis" in the poet as a man of his time, marking a development from Florio's Montaigne. "Hamlet in his meditations is almost a more intense projection of one aspect of the brooding inquisitiveness of Montaigne."[9] (Eliot says "almost" because Shakespeare is not *just* representative of his age in its relation to Montaigne. He also brings something quite personal to bear on the play.)

In another talk Donne is presented as "a man of thought," "of a more mature intellectual generation" than the earlier Elizabethan prose writers, yet a writer whose prose is essentially formed on Shakespearean poetry. Donne "imports" into prose two qualities of Shakespeare's blank verse and of the very best of his contemporaries in the drama: "a curious knowledge of the human heart, and a stateliness of phrase and image hitherto possible only in verse." The prose appeals to "an audience educated in verbal beauty by the Shakespearean drama."[10] Intellect, the historical stage of sensibility, and Shakespeare's poetry are very much at one in these considerations; the "curious knowledge of the human heart" is at one with the "stateliness of phrase and image." In

"Thinking in Verse" Eliot states that the finest poetry under Elizabeth is in the plays, "the profoundest thought and feeling of the age." And he speaks of the intellectual lyric in Donne as developing from "the complications of thought and feeling" in Elizabethan dramatic blank verse (as was suggested in "The Metaphysical Poets," without Eliot's bearing down so much on the question of intellectual development).[11] Shakespeare takes his place in an historical development of mind and sensibility—inevitably in the form of his poetry.

In the "Dante" essay of 1929 Eliot quotes two Shakespeare passages—the "temple-haunting martlet" lines from *Macbeth* and "She looks like sleep," as earlier noted. Here Eliot focuses on Shakespeare's peculiarity, the entirely individual quality of his poetry, where there is yet nothing of excess or self-indulgence. In trying to describe the quality of universality in Dante's language, its relatively easy translatability, Eliot points by contrast to the *Macbeth* passage and its "combination of intelligibility and remoteness" (*SE*, p. 203). The passage has an intellectual content that is graspable, yet this is subsistent in the series of exotic English words. The intention of the *Antony* passage is "expansive rather than intensive, to *add* to what you see (either on the stage or in your imagination)" (p. 205). Shakespeare's poetry takes us beyond what his material might seem to propose, rather than "intensifying" the proposal with what is "explanatory," as in Dante. ("Between men who could make such inventions as these there can be no question of greater or less" [p. 206].) Finally, Eliot compares Dante's Ulysses episode ("Inferno," XXVI) with Tennyson's "Ulysses" and praises Dante's greater "simplification." Tennyson has to "force" his effects. He is too "poetical." "Only Shakespeare can be so 'poetical' without giving any effect of overloading, or distracting us from the main issue: 'Put up your bright swords or the dew will rust them'" (p. 210). Shakespeare is peculiarly poetical, but necessarily so—we have in every step he takes us the sense of presence of the "main issue."

Eliot's remarks on Shakespeare's language amount to an insistence that the larger dramatic issues found in Shakespeare exist in the fabric of the poetry. The poetry is our point of direct contact and our final appeal. Eliot will himself talk about larger dramatic issues in Shakespeare during the twenties. But it is clear to anyone who reads him widely that he is extrapolating, so to speak, from direct experience of the poetry. He is speaking in general terms because it is the only way to speak, the only way to point to and be helpful about what is virtually a sensuous experience of words. Eliot's direct remarks on the language help to keep the more general remarks on drama in proportion to the primary experience. Eliot's criticism needs to be read whole (or diverse parts of it need to be read together).

The Created Character

Eliot's thoughts on character creation take in what the dramatist puts of himself into the character; what constitutes an aesthetic achievement in this area and how Shakespeare's achievement is to be distinguished from other successful sorts; and what the relation is between the audience and the created character on stage. This thinking leads naturally to that on the whole "poetic vision" of the drama and how it is conveyed to the audience.

In the "Ben Jonson" essay Eliot elaborates a theory of character creation as "the filling in of an outline." This, of course, amounts to the spinning out of a certain kind of poetry. He explains that Shakespeare's characters seem to differ from those of Jonson simply because of a greater complicatedness within the same aesthetic procedure of filling in an outline. Eliot begins speaking of the prologue of Sylla's ghost in *Catiline* (which he quotes): "This is the . . . creative Jonson. Without concerning himself with the character of Sulla . . . Jonson makes Sylla's ghost, while the words are spoken, a living and terrible force. . . . What Jonson has done here is not merely a fine speech. It is the careful, precise filling in of a strong and simple outline. . . ." What we have is not the character Sulla, but "Sylla's ghost"; and the words perfectly express this new thing: "there is a definite artistic emotion which demands expression at that length" (*SE,* p. 130). Here, and in ensuing remarks on other characters and the nature of Jonson's "creative" satire, Eliot makes clear that the center of character creation in this drama is the grasp of "a definite artistic emotion," which the dramatist spins out in dramatic speech, doing everything that is necessary to recreate the emotion fully, thus giving the sense of filling in a definite outline. (And it is not creation in a fantasy world: the Spirit of Envy in *Poetaster* is "a real and living person. It is not human life that informs envy and Sylla's ghost, but it is energy of which human life is only another variety.")

Having said this much, Eliot distinguishes both Shakespeare and Jonson from an altogether different kind of character creation: "The characters of Jonson, of Shakespeare, perhaps of all the greatest drama, are drawn in positive and simple outlines. They may be filled in, and by Shakespeare they are filled in, by much detail or many shifting aspects; but a clear and sharp and simple form remains through these" (p. 131). The characters of Shakespeare and Jonson are contrasted to Flaubert's Frédéric Moreau and, to a degree, characters of Molière, where a "negative definition" prevails: character is built up of precise observations (on the creator's part) of the recognizable, actual world. The audience must refer to that world or "the figure dissolves" (p. 132). Considered *relative* to this "negative definition," the procedure of characterization in Shakespeare and Jonson is one where a "form" remains, this form being a "definite artistic emotion," something created and new, held clearly in mind and worked out in poetry, organizing the details that make up the poetry.

From here on in the essay (which is, of course, chiefly concerned with the art of Jonson) Eliot takes pains to distinguish Jonson's character creation from Shakespeare's, while holding to the idea that both dramatists work within the overall aesthetic procedure that has been explained. Speaking of the whole design of Jonson's plays and the indissolubility of the character from the created scene and entire character network, Eliot notes: "The characters of Shakespeare are such as might exist in different circumstances than those in which Shakespeare sets them" (p. 132). Further: "Whereas in Shakespeare the effect is due to the way in which the characters *act upon* one another, in Jonson it is given by the way the characters *fit in* with each other" (p. 133). We can imagine Shakespeare's characters in a different setting from what we are given. And they act and react, making a difference to one another; that is, they *change*. Shakespeare is able to give us a sense of more being there in the character than is shown at any point or even in the whole play—what Shakespeare shows us of the characters "has not exhausted their possibilities" (p. 132). Presumably, the sense of unseen "possibilities" in the character helps us to credit the phenomenon of reacting and changing, to comprehend it and believe in it. A character who changes must also be one who seems *able to* change.

Eliot devotes a good deal of the essay to an explanation of this "three-dimensionality" of Shakespeare's characters (Gregory Smith's term for them, which appears in the book on Jonson that Eliot is reviewing), while insisting that Jonson's characters are not just products of the intellect. Shakespeare, Donne (presumably, we are to think of the dramatic voice), and some of the Jacobean dramatists are said to have "a depth, a third dimension . . . Their words have often a network of tentacular roots reaching down to the deepest terrors and desires" (p. 135). The words of these poets, what they use to create character or a consistent speaking voice, suggest the inarticulate depths of personality. Our depths, as audience, answer to the poets' depths. In Jonson there is "a kind of power" "animating" characters, "which comes from below the intellect." But it is the same kind of power that animates characters of Petronius, Rabelais, and Dickens (comparison with Marlowe has already been made in the essay). A kind of "fictive life" distinguishes these characters from those of Shakespeare: Barabas is not Shylock; Epicure Mammon not Falstaff; Faustus not Macbeth (p. 136). The difference is one of a relative simplicity as opposed to complicatedness (Shakespeare fills in his "outline" with "much detail or many shifting aspects"). But besides this there is a difference in temperament— Shakespeare's penchant for suggesting "possibilities" in the character opposes the Jonsonian farcical disposition to make a certain world of which the character is only a part.

Near the end of the essay Eliot offers a comprehensive theory to preserve the distinctions that are there and to obviate the temptation to make those that are not there. He brings us back to the initial idea of filling in an outline, holding to a "definite artistic emotion" in the writing of the speeches.

> The creation of a work of art, we will say the creation of a character in a drama, consists in the process of transfusion of the personality, or, in a deeper sense, the life, of the author into the character . . . Now, we may say . . . that Falstaff or a score of Shakespeare's

characters have a "third dimension" that Jonson's have not. This will mean . . . that Shakespeare's represent a more complex tissue of feelings and desires, as well as a more supple, a more susceptible temperament. [p. 137]

(This last point, of a "supple," "susceptible" temperament, may account for Shakespeare's ability to create a situation where the characters "act upon" one another; he is highly sensitive to the human disposition to react to things and be changed.)

Falstaff is not only the roast Manningtree ox with the pudding in his belly; he also "grows old," and, finally his nose is as sharp as a pen. He was perhaps the *satisfaction* of more, and of more complicated feelings; and perhaps he was, as the great tragic characters must have been, the offspring of deeper, less apprehensible feelings . . . than those of Jonson. [p. 137]

The difference with Shakespeare is "his susceptibility to a greater range of emotion, and emotion deeper and more obscure" (p. 137). Much as we are told in "Tradition and the Individual Talent," the artist begins with his own life, which involves depths not articulable except as "transfused" into the work of art. In creating the dramatic character the artist seizes on a "definite artistic emotion," what identifies Falstaff overall as Falstaff, or Sylla's ghost as Sylla's ghost. The definite artistic emotion determines—organizes—the writing out of the speeches and actions, the filling in of the outline. Into this outline may go words that suggest depths or complexities of feeling. Into the outline go *various* defined aspects—Falstaff as roast Manningtree ox, as one who "grows old," and so on. And into the outline goes the shifting of defined aspects of character so that the character changes, is "acted upon" by other characters. The dramatist takes hold of a definite artistic emotion, presumably, because it organizes, or permits, the feelings in himself—the "details"—that are asking to be articulated. Shakespeare does not transcribe life or himself but, like Jonson, creates a new thing, determined by an artistic idea that stands in relation to life as an outline does to its contents. Falstaff is not miraculously a real man on paper or on the stage; for all the real life contained in him, as in Macbeth or Shylock, he is finally an artistic "living force."

The "Massinger" essay reinforces points about the character as a newly created, and unified, entity and about the artist's transmutation of himself into the work of art, the character. Eliot notes that "a character, to be living, must be conceived from some emotional unity. A character is not to be composed of scattered observations of human nature, but of parts which are felt together . . . A 'living' character is not necessarily 'true to life.' It is a person whom we can see and hear, whether he be true or false to human nature as we know it" (*SE*, p. 188). To be "living" is to be conceived and worked out in detail from a "definite artistic emotion." The conception "from some emotional unity," the "parts [being] felt together," amounts to the artist's grasp of the definite artistic emotion, his working strictly in accord with it. The person "whom we can see and hear" is not the person we already know in life, but one we accept as a "person," however new and strange. Moreover, the creator of character needs not "knowledge of motives" or "understanding"—the intellectual equipment to construct character—but "keen sensibility" and "awareness." This sensibility and awareness exist not to make "observations of human nature," but to see in life, and in the artist's self, what it is that can be transfused into art, a creation "conceived from . . . unity," having the quality of a "person."

Eliot criticizes Massinger for working too much with conventions of value and behavior, which create, as it were, a literary remove from life in his characters and their actions. Eliot instances Middleton's *Changeling*, where Beatrice rails against Deflores, and the end of *Othello* as the thing to be desired in drama. "The emotion of Othello in Act V is the emotion of a man who discovers that the worst part of his own soul has been exploited by some one more clever than he; it is this emotion carried by the writer to a very high degree of intensity" (pp. 188–89). The last act of *Othello* is mercifully not something we are likely to have seen in life. "The man who discovers that the worst part of his soul has been exploited," this anyone might have seen or known. Shakespeare has "carried" this emotion (and the plot and events at the end are part of the "carrying") "to a very high degree of intensity." The art exists in that "intensification."

Later in the "Massinger" essay Eliot speaks of "three-dimensionality" and what the artist puts of himself into his characters. As in the "Jonson" essay, Marlowe and Jonson are distinguished from Shakespeare: the characters of Marlowe and Jonson are "slight" beside Shakespeare's; Falstaff has a "third dimension" that Epicure Mammon lacks (p. 192). But also as before, Eliot insists that Marlowe and Jonson have transfused real feeling into the created work— theirs is "the transformation of a personality into a personal work of art" (p. 192); it is just that their two-dimensional way with character suits their Petronian-Rabelaisian disposition. They are simpler than Shakespeare in what they begin with in themselves, wanting to transform it. But they have integrity as artists equal to Shakespeare's; they are whole from man to work (where Massinger as artist is mired in conventions, the secondhand—"his personality hardly exists" [p. 192]). Eliot quotes the Remy de Gourmont passage that begins, "La vie est un dépouillement," stating of Flaubert and his books, "il se transvasait goutte à gouette." He goes on to say that Shakespeare, and to a degree Jonson, Marlowe, and Keats, ought to be put in this category—"they *se transvasaient goutte à gouette*" (pp. 192–93). The character as "a person whom we can see and hear," "not necessarily 'true to life,'" carries to the "intensity" of art—where a "definite artistic emotion," an "outline," obtains— real feelings from life and from the personality of the artist.

After the "Massinger" essay, in 1921, Eliot writes again of character creation, this time with attention to the audience and its response, in a piece for

Wyndham Lewis's *Tyro,* "The Romantic Englishman, the Comic Spirit, and the Function of Criticism." This little essay is a complaint against contemporary theater and concerns itself with the larger possibilities of dramatic characters of the past and what they mean to audiences. It contains statements about character creation that accord with Eliot's previous thinking: "The 'mythic' character [the subject of the essay] is not composed of abstract qualities; it is a point of view, transmuted to importance; it is made by the transformation of the actual by imaginative genius. 'Volpone' . . . criticizes humanity by intensifying wickedness."[12] Again, there is a beginning in real feeling or observation of the real, then a transformation in art to the realm of "imagination" and "intensity." But for the most part, Eliot is concerned now with the audience rather than with the artist or the created character.

Eliot sketches out a view of the audience and its relation to characters as a function of a certain idealism, though by no means a crude or sentimental idealism. He extends this view to the audience's experience of serious as well as comic drama, and literary as well as theatrical creations. Eliot posits a "romantic Englishman" as the typical audience member, who wants in dramatic creations a certain idealization of himself; there exists a general "myth" created by various characters. Sir Giles Overreach (who is discussed favorably in the "Massinger" essay), Squire Western, and Tom Jones are instanced—"different contributions by distinguished mythmakers to the chief myth which the Englishman has built about himself." Falstaff is mentioned, though he is said to be "elevated above the myth to dwell on Olympus, more than a national character." Shakespeare is distinguished as being universal in contrast to the other English writers, while he is yet a part of the moral-aesthetic phenomenon that is being noticed (Charlie Chaplin is similarly distinguished later in the essay).

Despite the invocation of prose fiction, the theater is said to be "naturally the best platform for the myth," but the present-day theater "affords . . . singularly little relief," its characters being "a poor showing." "The Englishman with a craving for the ideal . . . famishes in the stalls of the modern theater." Eliot explains the "craving": "Man desires to see himself on the stage, more admirable, more forceful, more villainous, more comical, more despicable—and more much else—than he actually is." The range of desires here—with that "more much else"—suggests that the idealization is not something simple, crude, or sentimental. The audience positively wants something and is ready to be led into new regions by the artist. A Giles Overreach, much more a Falstaff, will answer a craving; but the character is not something the audience will have imagined precisely in advance. Eliot says that at present only the cinema (here is where he mentions Chaplin) and the music hall give us a "realization" of what is wanted. He lists the names of Marie Lloyd and a number of other music-hall comedians, claiming they "provide fragments of a possible English myth." "They effect the Comic Purgation. The romantic Englishman, feeling in himself the possibility of being as funny as these people, is purged of unsatisfied desire, transcends himself, and unconsciously lives the myth, seeing life in the light of imagination." Feeling possibility in oneself, transcending oneself, "unconsciously living" another life, having for the regard of life itself the benefit of "the light of imagination"—this is the substance of the relation of the audience to dramatic characters. (On the death of Marie Lloyd in 1922, Eliot published an article about her in both the *Dial* and *The Criterion,* which he reprints in *Selected Essays.* He speaks of her "giving expression to the life of the audience . . . raising it to a kind of art." Her audience had "recognition of the fact that she embodied the virtues which they genuinely most respected in private life.")[13]

Eliot concludes "The Romantic Englishman" by turning to the moral dimension of what goes on between the dramatic character and the audience; he asserts that this event is important to life, while in another sense it does not modify life. Eliot says that the process that goes on between artist or character and audience must be "unconscious." Either the performance of the music-hall comedian or the range of persons Jonson puts upon the stage contains "a compliment and a criticism" of the audience. But the audience is not aware of the "compliment and criticism" as such; conceivably, neither is the artist. The audience is "willing to accept [its] own ideal," but "only unconsciously." Its thinking is on the level of "fun"; Eliot says of the music-hall comedian that "in all probability" he must think of what he is doing as "fun" too—the proposition is not hard to extend to the playwright as well. Here Eliot brings up the "serious stage," saying that serious characters are currently "confected of abstract qualities . . . to which we are supposed to respond with the proper abstract emotions." But the true "myth" is not composed of abstract qualities; the "transformation of the actual by imaginative genius" is not a matter of conceptualization, asking of the audience a response as if to a conceptualization. Eliot states the paradox: "The myth is imagination and it is also criticism, and the two are one." There is criticism in fact, but it is not regardable as such. Eliot says of the seventeenth century that "its drama is a criticism of humanity far more serious than its conscious moral judgments." *Volpone* amounts conceptually to a "showing" that wickedness is punished; its real "criticism" lies in "intensifying" wickedness.

Finally, the myth, for all its importance to the life of the audience, does not change life as conceptual discourse, say a sermon, is supposed to do. Here Eliot speaks of what he will later call the pure "consolation" of art, which he will discuss in essays (notably "Shakespeare and the Stoicism of Seneca") where he worries about meaning in Shakespeare. He says now: "The Seventeenth Century populace was not appreciably modified by its theater . . . The myth is based upon reality, but does not alter it." Eliot feels that the artist and the audience are involved with reality; both dwell upon a coherence made of reality—the character, a "definite artistic emotion," an "outline" filled in. There is "criticism" of which the audience is aware at an "unconscious" level.

But the whole experience, nourishing to the audience's "desire" and in a sense to its intellect, does not amount to an exchange of practicable ideas. There is change for the audience in the experience, but regarded from a certain point of view of action in life, it is change within stasis.

"The Romantic Englishman" shows Eliot moving easily from prose fiction to drama, music-hall performance to scripted play. He implies that reading about Squire Western has the essential qualities of dramatic experience, the same experience felt when we read the speeches of Shakespeare or Jonson, or see their characters on the stage, or indeed enjoy a performance of Marie Lloyd or Little Tich. Certainly, Eliot has said a great deal (and he will say more) to enforce the point that the phrase, the word, is primary in drama; our concentration upon the word makes possible the full resonance of drama. At the same time, in this essay and in many to come (he will recommend Granville-Barker's criticism, for example), Eliot shows himself sensitive to the purely theatrical dimension of drama. The fact is—it becomes a mark of his criticism of drama—that for Eliot there is no exclusiveness between the literary and theatrical considerations of drama. Reading prose fiction may be an essentially dramatic experience. And the performer in the theater, even the music-hall performer, may engage the same values and ideals of the audience, the craving to live another life, as does the most considered poetic text.

This easy movement between literary and theatrical considerations is continued in later essays. In "Wilkie Collins and Dickens" (1927) Eliot writes of Dickens's characters as having "that kind of reality which is almost supernatural, which hardly seems to belong to the character by natural right, but seems rather to descend upon him by a kind of inspiration or grace." This statement is reminiscent of those made about the "myth" and idealization in "The Romantic Englishman." Eliot goes on: "Dickens's figures belong to poetry, like figures of Dante or Shakespeare, in that a single phrase, either by them or about them, may be enough to set them wholly before us" (*SE,* p. 411). One example Eliot gives is the reference to Cleopatra: "I saw her once, / Hop forty paces through the public street." Clearly, we are concerned in these remarks with the character as a person, a life to be seen in relation to our own lives— but be it Dickens, Shakespeare, or Dante, the mode of presentation makes no essential difference.

In the essay on Marie Lloyd already mentioned Eliot comments that the audience member who saw Marie Lloyd and joined in the chorus was actually "performing" and working in "collaboration" with the artist. Further, such collaboration is "necessary in all art," most obviously in drama (*SE,* p. 407). Eliot here focuses on the rapport of performer with audience in the unscripted music-hall situation where the audience actually sings. But the engagement of the audience member with the character should be extended in our consideration, not only to "dramatic art" in general, but to "*all* art" (my emphasis), where, presumably, only the writer, or the composer of music, or whatever artist we may think of, may be seen in the position of the dramatic character. This is an extraordinary statement. "Collaboration of the audience with the artist" is finally all the point. The discussion of music hall and drama seems just a particular focusing of attention upon the manifestation of a deeper principle. The statement, like so much of Eliot's criticism when looked at closely, *emphasizes* something we can enter into—here the music-hall situation and more broadly drama—but does not set up exclusive categories. A little thought takes us beyond the immediate situation to the abiding issue of the very nature of art and the audience's relation to it.

The Whole "Poetic Vision" and the Audience

Already, in the remarks in "The Romantic Englishman" on the element of "criticism" in drama and on the ultimate effect upon the audience, Eliot is getting away from the consideration of the dramatic character by himself and moving toward consideration of the play as a whole—his old interest. In a number of essays beginning with "The Duchess of Malfi" and going on through the twenties, he explains a view of poetic drama as the conveying of a "poetic vision" to the audience. It is a procedure from artist to audience that involves concentration upon the word and is at the same time fully theatrical.

The substance of the "poetic vision" is not a philosophy or a practicable idea; it is best described as a "point of view" or "world," something "rich and strange"—Eliot picks up the tag from Ariel's song in *The Tempest,* so important to the whole transformation theme in *The Waste Land.* The form the "poetic vision" takes is that of a "rhythm," a term Eliot defines delicately, intending not so much to propose a category as to direct our attention to something. There are a number of analogies drawn between drama and the ballet, which Eliot frequently mentions enjoying in these years. And the audience of drama is said to be involved in the work as it is in ritual. In a review of a production of *King Lear* Eliot describes the proper open response for the audience. In other essays he remarks on the presence of comedy and tragedy together in Shakespeare and on the nature of his grasp of the "real" and the "typical"—components of the whole "rich and strange" "poetic vision."

In "The Duchess of Malfi" (1919), which reviews a Phoenix Society production, Eliot complains that the actors "make" their parts, missing the proper style, "interpreting." He takes the occasion to spell out what poetic drama really is. He begins the article by remarking on our loss of the reality of Shakespeare by, it is implied, a sort of intellectual failure—a point close to those of the early essays: "Years of patient labor have so purified, transmogrified, and debased Shakespeare that several of his plays can be produced before audiences of the most civilized householders and shareholders in the world."[14] Our debased notion of Shakespeare plays into the hands of the "interpreting" actors; later in the essay Shakespeare is associated with Webster in the complaint that the poetry is obstructed by the ways of modern theater (pp. 36, 38).

Here Eliot moves to a general consideration of drama. He insists on distinguishing the "acting play" from closet drama and says that the lines of *The Duchess* are "meant to be spoken." "The significance of the best poetry in 'The Duchess of Malfi' is that it is dramatic poetry" (p. 36). This kind of drama, Shakespeare's or others', is thus seen to be an event of the theater. Eliot speaks of the successes and failures of the Phoenix Society with various kinds of scenes (pp. 36–38), concluding: "We want the enjoyment of spoken poetry across the stage, the design of a scene, of costume, of movement, and the excitement of something very fine taking place before a number of people" (p. 38). It is poetry and at the same time theater—speech, design, movement—and the effect of it upon the audience is "excitement," the sense of "something very fine taking place."

Just below this Eliot distinguishes poetic drama as being "literary art" in opposition to most modern drama, like that of Ibsen (to whom Eliot is much kinder later) or fashionable entertainment drama. Of the usual modern production of *Hamlet* Eliot says that "only the plot is Shakespeare's"; the words, as "poetry," are lost (p. 38). Eliot wants "poetry" to be "transmitted" (p. 39). This is what the drama of Shakespeare or Webster is meant to be and what a production now ought to achieve. With some praise for *The Dynasts,* Eliot says that the objective of poetic drama is "to get a poetic vision on to the stage," "to make some intense effect carry across to the stalls and gallery, to convey a dominant tone. To obtain, with verse, an effect as immediate and direct as that of the best ballet" (p. 39). (Eliot sounds somewhat like Yeats in his writing for *Samhain*—for example, "The Reform of the Theater"—early in the century. But Eliot does not mention Yeats's effort in the theater until pieces on drama in the mid-1930s.) Poetry, the word, is central, but the purpose of poetry in drama, whether spoken in the theater or simply read—Eliot is clear at the start that "acting drama" is more "readable" than closet drama (p. 36)—the purpose of the poetry is to form a whole, a "poetic vision" characterizable as an "intense effect," "a dominant tone," "an effect . . . immediate and direct." If there is speech, design, movement, it will be essentially poetic—presumably, bound to the word and formative of the whole, the "effect."

Eliot refines these points in a number of essays over the next few years, trying to describe the "poetic vision" or "effect" he sees at the heart of drama. In "The Poetic Drama," a review of Middleton Murry's *Cinnamon and Angelica* in 1920, with general thoughts on the problems facing the would-be writer of poetic drama, we are told that the poet–dramatist "is impelled both by a desire to give form to something in his mind, and by a desire that a certain desirable emotional state should be produced."[15] The "poetic vision" is the achieved "form" in drama that comes from sources in the poet, the man (again, we are close to "Tradition and the Individual Talent"). The "poetic vision" in its effect upon the audience is an "emotional state."

Later in "The Poetic Drama" Eliot speaks enviously, as he will do again in "The Possibility of a Poetic Drama,"[16] of the Greek and Elizabethan theaters, where there is a form given by the society, allowing the artist to concentrate on what he would make of the given, or on the individual "form" of a particular play. The artist can go far in one direction because he has a certain "co-operation" ready in his audience, "one means almost the temper of the age . . . a preparedness, a habit, on the part of the public, to respond in a predictable way, however crudely, to certain stimuli."[17] Eliot instances Elizabethan "Death-and-Worms" and Greek "Fate" and concludes, "commonplaces they were, but capable of indefinite refinement." This theater was not only conventional but also popular. Murry's play is too *deliberately* poetic; "he is not held down by the necessity of *entertaining* an audience cruder than himself," a necessity that gives the "dramatic structure" as opposed to the artist's special "emotional structure." The given "dramatic structure" allows the artist to concentrate on the "emotional structure" he would create, without violating the nature of human speech and action (p. 635). Thus, the popular nature of the theater is at once a boon and the condition *in spite of which* the artist achieves his special work. Near the end of the essay Eliot returns to what is its chief concern, the nature of that "special work," the particular form in any play that is developed from the "something in mind" of the individual poet, the "poetic vision" that is the play. This, he states, is what Shakespeare was able to achieve: "In the middle of a rowdy seventeenth-century playhouse pit the thought of Shakespeare, the feeling and the shuddering personal experience of Shakespeare moved solitary and unsoiled; solitary and free as the thought of Spinoza in his study or Montaigne in his tower" (ibid.).

In "The Possibility of a Poetic Drama" (1920), again concerned with the current theater situation, Eliot speaks about the given form of the Elizabethan drama, which gave the blank verse "a subtlety and consciousness . . . an intellectual power"; Shakespeare has as a given "a crude form, capable of indefinite refinement" (*SW,* pp. 62–63). And Eliot is still aware of the need for a sort of compromise with popular dictates. Attempts to overcome the public's vulgar expectations of its stage—such as what the public looks for in an actor—do not succeed (Eliot refers to the current use of masks and other new "conventions").

> Meddling with nature seldom succeeds . . . Possibly the majority of attempts to confect a poetic drama have begun at the wrong end; they have aimed at the small public which wants "poetry" . . . The Elizabethan drama was aimed at a public which wanted *entertainment* of a crude sort, but would *stand* a good deal of poetry; our problem should be to take a form of entertainment, and subject it to the process which would leave it a form of art. [pp. 69–70]

But Eliot's real purpose in the "Possibility" essay is to describe what the drama must be, however it may be helped along toward that goal by its society: "Permanent literature is always a presentation; either a presentation of thought, or a presentation of feeling by a statement of events in human action or objects in the external world . . . Aristotle presents thought, stripped to the essential structure, and he is a great *writer*. The *Agamemnon* or *Macbeth* is equally a statement, but of events" (pp. 64–65). A "presentation," a "statement," the "something in mind" being made into "events in human action"—this account, reminiscent of the "objective correlative," is what has now become of the "poetic vision" in Eliot's thinking (Hardy's *Dynasts* is again commended in a footnote as being "essentially an attempt to present a vision" [p. 66]).

With his general designation "permanent literature" and then, after what has been quoted, the use of *Education sentimentale* as an example, Eliot shows again an ease of movement between the "literary" and the "dramatic." His primary concern is the presentation of feeling and the eliciting of a response, not whether the audience is watching a play or reading a book. Eliot quotes Aristotle to emphasize the importance of "incident," "action," and "life" ("and life consists in action") as opposed to "undigested" ideas in drama (p. 67). He speaks of Flaubert's successful "transmutation" of ideas, what was his "something in mind," we may say: "The attitude of Flaubert toward the small bourgeois is transformed in *Education sentimentale*. It has there become so identified with the reality that you can no longer say what the reality is" (p. 68). The conclusion: "The essential is to get upon the stage this precise statement of life which is at the same time a point of view, a world—a world which the author's mind has subjected to a complete process of simplification" (p. 68). The "poetic vision" is not an "idea"; but in "events," in a created "reality," there is a "point of view," a "world." With the growing series of terms, we begin to realize that Eliot's real effort in these essays is to point to something, to direct our attention, and to prevent us from making certain conceptual mistakes—indeed, perhaps to prevent our conceptualizing or categorizing at all. Eliot is directing us to what cannot be precisely named. A further description, another indication of the reality of the "poetic vision," is found in some remarks on the ballet in Eliot's third "London Letter" (1921): "The ballet will probably be one of the influences forming a new drama, if a new drama ever comes . . . what is needed of art is a simplification of current life into something rich and strange."[18] The "simplification" of drama that was desiderated of new drama in the "Possibility" essay, and attributed there to *Macbeth*, the *Agamemnon,* and other work, is now to be known as "something rich and strange."

Just as Eliot does not distinguish sharply between the "literary" and the "dramatic," so in his concern with the "poetic vision" he does not draw a firm conceptual line between the achieved work of the artist (the formal aspect) and the "effect" upon the audience. The analogies he makes with the ballet, taken altogether, enforce this unwillingness to draw a line. In the third "London Letter" Eliot appeals to what he hopes will be admitted as the "rich and strange" in Diaghilev's presentations; what Eliot has in mind here is the artist's achieved "form," the achieved "transmutation" of the original "something in mind." In the earlier "Duchess of Malfi" essay the ballet was appealed to for its "effect . . . immediate and direct," the more experiential side of the theatrical event. In a 1920 essay called "Modern Tendencies in Poetry" Eliot also appeals to the ballet as showing that "we *can* pass an evening in a theater and have some intense experience"; after the ballet, we will not accept boring theater. Today we experience pleasure in *Hamlet* or *Measure for Measure* more in reading them than in going to the theater. In Shakespeare's day, Eliot postulates, one would go to the theater and still have one's "solitary pleasure"—coming into contact, we may put it, with Shakespeare's special thought, feeling, and "shuddering personal experience."[19] Here in the "Modern Tendencies" essay the ballet is appealed to for the "intensity" of the experience of the audience. But the essay as a whole, coming down to a complaint about poetry of the present, is an extended discussion of transmutation reminiscent of "Tradition and the Individual Talent." By the time the essay mentions the ballet and Shakespeare, it has been made quite clear that "intensity" in the audience's experience is simply the other side of the coin of the artist's objectification of his original feeling, an objectification amounting in part to an "appeal to the senses" of the audience.[20] ("Modern Tendencies" and the 1921 *Chapbook* essay "Prose and Verse" offer more extended treatments of the subject matter of "Tradition and the Individual Talent"; the two uncollected essays make much clearer what the famous "Tradition" essay is talking about. As I have noted, "Prose and Verse" cites the Gravediggers scene in *Hamlet* as an example of perfectly achieved "poetry," in connection with Remy de Gourmont's dictum that style preserves literature.)

Eliot has much to say about the effect of drama on the audience and about the audience's proper involvement with drama. He feels, in part, that drama is, or ought to be, like ritual. In a *Criterion* piece in 1923, "Dramatis Personae," on the current variety of acting styles to be found, and with praise for the "abstract" and Massine as a model, Eliot proposes the ideal: "Instead of pretending that the stage gesture is a copy of reality, let us adopt a literal untruth, a thoroughgoing convention, a ritual. For the stage—not only in its remote origins, but always—is a ritual, and the failure of the contemporary stage to satisfy the craving for ritual is one of the reasons why it is not a living art." Eliot goes on to praise Chaplin in the cinema: "The egregious merit of Chaplin is that he has escaped in his own way from the realism of the cinema and invented a *rhythm*."[21] The ritual-like nature of drama consists in its "invention" of a "rhythm," its transmutation of whatever feeling or intellectual substance it may contain into a "rhythm" that answers to an audience's "craving for ritual." The "rhythm," like the "poetic vision" itself, is not easily described or translated into the terms of one or two familiar categories. What this essay makes clear about "rhythm" is that it has to do with consistency and with the change into art, the making abstract, in a sense, of what is not art—ideas familiar in Eliot. And Eliot makes clear that the "craving" to which rhythm answers is not a detached or "aesthetic" one, but a matter of strong feeling: "We can only guess at the scheme of what we grope for by inference from our perceptions, from observation of any instant on the stage which has aroused an hitherto dormant feeling" (p. 305). To "arouse feeling" is the purpose of the achieved "rhythm"; the achieved rhythm doing *this* is the basis of the analogy to ritual.

In "The Beating of a Drum" (1923), an essay on the Elizabethan Fool and the convergence of the comic and the tragic in Shakespeare, Eliot cites Butcher on Aristotle: "'Poetry, music, and dancing constitute in Aristotle a group by themselves, their common element being imitation by means of rhythm—rhythm which admits of being applied to words, sounds, and the movements of the body.'"[22] Rhythm exists in Shakespeare, but present-day "interpreters" "suppress" it. Aristotle was "accustomed to dramatic performances only in rhythmic form" and never had to answer "how far the catharsis could be effected by the moral or intellectual significance of the play *without* its verse form and proper declamation" (p. 12). Catharsis, a reaction in deep feeling, is essential in drama; "rhythm," what drama is if it is fully itself—"verse form and proper declamation"—is the means to drama's end. Eliot has mentioned Cornford's *The Origin of Attic Comedy* earlier in the essay (p. 11), and now he reminds us that "the drama was originally ritual." He goes on to call ritual "essentially a dance" and to say that dance, like the beating of a drum, is something people were perhaps originally just seized with a desire to do, only later finding "reasons" for it. Shakespeare, Eliot says, still has—if properly performed or properly taken, it is implied—the action that one "desires to do," "rhythm" as a transmutation of any "moral or intellectual significance" (p. 12). Eliot does not distinguish between the spectator and the created character or performer. We are reminded of "The Romantic Englishman," which describes the audience member who "unconsciously lives" the life of the created character, whether seen on the stage or read in a book.

At the end of 1923, in a review of poems by Marianne Moore, Eliot confirms the sense he has given that "rhythm" is a matter of the whole "form" that pervades every detail, not a technical or measurable matter. "Rhythm . . . is always the real pattern in the carpet, the scheme of organization of thought, feeling, and vocabulary, the way in which everything comes together."[23] After attempting to describe Marianne Moore's "new rhythm," Eliot says this does not amount to "an aristocratic art, emulating the condition of ritual" (as one critic, Glenway Wescott, suggests) for the reason that "*all* art emulates the condition of ritual. That is what it comes from and to that it must always return for nourishment" (p. 597). The "condition of ritual" is an appeal to a "desire," a more or less universal one, that is answered by a "rhythm" in the encompassing sense Eliot gives it.

Eliot has mentioned Cornford, and a word ought to be said about the relation of Eliot on ritual to the classical anthropologists of the period. The work of Jane Harrison, Gilbert Murray (referred to with Cornford in "The Beating of a Drum"), and Francis Cornford appeared from 1912 to 1914. They wrote on the development of Greek drama from seasonal ritual, the persistence of ritual patterns in the plays that we have, and the likely interest as-in-ritual the Greek audience would have taken in the plays.[24] These scholars make use of Frazer's *Golden Bough* (published between 1890 and 1915 in increments and new editions), which deals with a deep universal state of mind focused on the death and rebirth of the god, a mentality that underlies the religion and art of many times and places—a work Eliot frequently praises and expresses great interest in.[25] And the classicists often draw analogies to medieval and later European drama. Eliot read all this work for Josiah Royce's seminar at Harvard in 1913–14 when he was making a special study of the interpretation of primitive ritual. There are interesting connections between these writers and Eliot's thinking on various literary matters, though he is critical in his seminar paper of the new classical anthropology for being *overly* interpretive, bringing too much of ideas into the pure act.[26] But Eliot does not, in the 1923 essays on drama, take over a whole view of ritual or of ritual-like drama from the classical anthropologists. He does not mention the fertility pattern, or the Frazerian universal state of mind, or the dependence of drama as art upon earlier patterns. Eliot's view is his own, particularly with his delicate development of the idea of "rhythm." He is to be understood only by looking at his own various explanations.

Eliot speaks of the reaction or involvement of the audience as something more than simple or trancelike. He has indicated as much in "The Romantic Englishman," where he talks about the audience member's living in imagination the life of the "mythic" character. In other essays Eliot speaks more of the reaction to the play as a whole, suggesting a deep stirring of the moral sensitivity that yet does not come to an alteration of practical life. In his second "London Letter" Eliot reviews the Phoenix Society *Volpone,* giving it high praise: "the most important theatrical event of the year in London," "suberbly carried out," "proceeding without a moment of tedium from end to end."[27] He defends the violence of Elizabethan plays and the Phoenix Society's refusal to admit any expurgation of indecencies, commenting that "the sense of relief, in hearing the indecencies of Elizabethan and Restoration drama, leaves one a better and a stronger man" (pp. 686–87). This enthusiasm for taking all that the Elizabethan play has to offer leads to reflection on Shakespeare similar to that found in the "Duchess of Malfi" essay: "We do not know Shakespeare; we only know Sir J. Forbes-Robertson's Hamlet, and Irving's Shylock, and so on . . . Shakespeare . . . strained through the nineteenth century, has been dwarfed to the dimensions of a part for this or that actor" (p. 687). We have seen that Eliot's earliest remarks on Shakespeare attest to the poet's real overwhelmingness, despite what is said or thought about him. Now it is suggested positively that Shakespeare has a range of violence and indecency that we open ourselves to in "relief."

In *The Criterion* in 1924 Eliot reviews the Phoenix Society *King Lear,* "the finest performance in the history of the Phoenix Society," notable for the "co-operation" of the actors with each other, their "harmony." "The collaboration of the actors in the storm scenes made this part of the play an event in a lifetime." The production, in short, had the virtue needed to convey the play as a whole. As for the quality of the play, Eliot states that *"King Lear* is a work of such immense power that it offends and scandalizes ordinary citizens of both sexes." This scandal is what Eliot noticed at the performance. He goes on to reflect on the literary culture of the day, which the *Volpone* review calls a product of the nineteenth century, and to reflect again on the question of reading versus acting:

> The play of *King Lear* can never be popular in a civilization so corrupted with literary culture that it resents what it cannot diminish. For there is a form of literary culture which shrinks from direct contact with a great work of art. In reading a play you can avoid this contact; you may talk about the play, or you may write about it, or you may read what has been written about it; but if you sit through a performance in a theater, you cannot attend to anything but the play itself.

And Eliot speaks of an "aversion for the work of art," a "preference for the derivative, the marginal," an "incapacity for surrender or allegiance to something outside of oneself."[28] Perhaps in our later time, when *King Lear* has indeed become popular, there is still a problem with diminishment of one sort or another; after all, as Eliot notes, *Hamlet* and *The Merchant of Venice* were sufficiently "popular" in the years around 1920.

The important point here is that what *Lear* offers is "immense power," a range of violence and indecency, we may say, likely to offend and scandalize. It offers an opportunity to the audience—we may presume the Elizabethan audience took the opportunity—for "direct contact," for single "attention," for "surrender" to something. What Eliot is asking of the audience—what he says the Shakespeare play is asking—is openness. The "poetic vision," perhaps including lives to be lived imaginatively, perhaps moral provocation, all of which is transmuted to a "rhythm," asks us not to think, at least in ways that we are accustomed to think, but rather to "attend," "surrender" ourselves. We can surrender to either reading or performance. When Eliot was seeing no good performances, he opted for reading—performance was usually a diminishment. Now, with the Phoenix *King Lear,* good performance provokes discomfort in the London audience; it does not permit the avoidance reading permits. The thing to be sought, with either reading or performance, is "direct contact."

In a number of essays of the early and middle 1920s Eliot gives a more detailed explanation of what he sees the "poetic vision" and its "effect" on the audience to consist of, particularly in Shakespeare. In "Andrew Marvell" (1921) he devotes considerable attention to that poet's "alliance of levity and seriousness (by which the seriousness is intensified)." This "alliance" amounts to a "sophistication of feeling," a "hold on human values, [a] firm grasp of human experience." Finally, it is "wisdom, cynical perhaps but untired." In a striking parenthesis Eliot notes that what he is talking about appears "in Shakespeare, a terrifying clairvoyance" (*SE*, pp. 255–56). The presence of the comic and tragic together in Shakespeare becomes one of Eliot's perpetual themes throughout his critical career. In the thirties and later he will go further with the idea of an implicit "wisdom" in this combination. In the twenties he insists merely on the copresence of the two moods as part of the dramatic vision Shakespeare presents, part of our experience in opening ourselves to this "world."

In "The Beating of a Drum" Eliot says that Shakespeare's most remarkable contributions to the line of Fools occur in the tragedies. He mentions the Fool in *Lear*, the Witches in *Macbeth*, Caliban, the Porter in *Macbeth*, and Antony in Pompey's Galley scene. With the first three examples there is an issue of "possessedness" or shamanism in combination with the comic, while "the Porter and Antony are Fools because they provide a contrast of mood which contributes to the seriousness of the situation." In pure comedy "this antithesis is attenuated." And Eliot concludes: "It is in tragedy, or in some form which is neither comedy nor tragedy, that the Fool . . . is best observed."[29] Eliot draws our attention to tragedy with the Fool, or to "some form which is neither comedy nor tragedy," as Shakespeare's medium for obtaining the uncanny effects of some plays, the intensified "seriousness" by "contrast" of others. He goes on to bring up Cornford and the theory of the development of comedy and tragedy out of a common form, an "original dramatic impulse"; it is a unified desire, as if to beat a drum, on which Shakespeare has still got a grasp.[30]

Other essays also discuss this idea. In a review of a complete edition of Shakespeare in 1926 Eliot declares that the division of the plays into comedy, tragedy, and history is "arbitrary" and bound to create confusion (other points of the review are that the canon has a unity and needs to be assimilated before one advances to questions of authorship, as in Robertson, and that it is dangerous to try to pin down the political opinions of Shakespeare).[31] In the "Middleton" essay (1927), when Eliot is faced with the problem of a seeming lack of personality in the work of Middleton, he remarks: "Between the tragedies and comedies of Shakespeare, and certainly between the tragedies and comedies of Jonson, we can establish a relation; we can see, for Shakespeare or Jonson, that each had in the end a personal point of view which can be called neither tragic nor comic" (*SE*, p. 141). And in the "Tourneur" essay (1930), speaking of the "tasteless" transitions (themselves "a kind of taste") from comic to tragic in Tourneur and Marston, Eliot draws a contrast with Webster and Shakespeare, where the farcical and tragic are "harmonious." The Porter scene in *Macbeth* is the great prototype (*SE*, pp. 163–64). Eliot has in mind a tragedy and comedy, each of which admits the mood of the other, or "some form which is neither comedy nor tragedy." The individual dramatist's "point of view" takes form in what is neither precisely comedy nor precisely tragedy. Between the "antithesis" of moods, as with the Porter in *Macbeth*, there is "harmony."

In the "Massinger" essay Eliot says that Shakespeare and Middleton in *The Changeling* derive "unique emotions," "permanent and substantial," from the conventions of conduct found in drama of the time; the great dramatist's concern is with the "personal and real emotion" that the conventions support and bring a "kind of order" to (*SE,* pp. 188–89). It is important to see that Eliot understands drama to occur not in a fantastic or conventional world, but in a world of actual emotions. He says that the "alliance of seriousness and levity" amounts to a "hold on human values," a "firm grasp of human experience." In this essay the great dramatist, unlike Massinger, is seen to deal with the conventions of conduct, "criticizing and informing them from his own experience" (p. 188).

To read through the "Massinger" essay is to see the connection between, on the one hand, closeness of word and object in the poetry of Shakespeare and the better dramatists, and, on the other hand, these dramatists' ability to obtain "permanent and substantial" emotions—indeed, the "living" character. The dramatist will succeed with emotion and characters if he is one for whom the use of language is a "development of feeling," for whom style reflects "a mode of perceiving, registering, and digesting." But the "object" or feeling in poetry is not something familiar we are referred back to, but a creation, what we *accept* as an object or feeling. The "living" character is not necessarily "true to life," but what we see and hear and *accept* as a living character. So the "permanent and substantial" emotion of a scene is not something the play copies from life, or refers us back to in life, but what the play compels us to accept as a permanent emotion. Eliot does not want to speak against the transmuting nature of the work of art—the emotion of *Othello* in act 5 is an "intensification" of what we may recognize from life, what has its beginning in Shakespeare the man. Eliot's point is a matter of emphasis. He wants to distinguish the drama of actual, if thoroughly created, emotion from that of "social abstractions" (p. 190).

Eliot returns to this emphasis on the "real" emotion in Shakespeare a number of times, conceiving of the real emotion as connected, alternatively, to the emotion of Shakespeare the man or to the observable world. In a 1923 essay on Donne's love poems Eliot claims it is "impossible . . . to isolate what is 'conventional' in Donne from what is individual"; a comparison is drawn to Shakespeare's sonnets. Eliot offers a dictum to account for, or to focus our attention upon, this delicate area between the personal and the literary: "With sincerity in the practical sense, poetry has little to do; the poet is responsible to a much more difficult consciousness and honesty."[32] This "difficult consciousness and honesty" is the way to transmute into art, with its *use* of convention, whatever of the person goes into art. The result has a quality of "personality" or "reality" by contrast with the purely conventional art of a Massinger. In a 1928 review of the Herford and Simpson *Ben Jonson* (first three volumes) Eliot quotes the editors approvingly to counter the idea of Jonson as isolated and "pseudo-classical." In Jonson, in Shakespeare, in many dramatists of the time, it is said, we get one common result: "'the drastic and humorous representation of the life of Elizabethan England.'"[33] We get in this drama not a pure literary world, but a "representation"—we might say a "transmutation"—of the life of a world of human beings in history. Finally, in the BBC talk on Donne's sermons, part of the large series on Elizabethan-Jacobean literature, Eliot says that Donne imports into prose two qualities found among his contemporaries only in the blank verse of Shakespeare and the best of the other dramatists: "a curious knowledge of the human heart, and a stateliness of phrase and image."[34] This remark reiterates the idea of the intimate connection of "knowledge" in literature (whether sermon or play) with the word itself, the quality of phrase and image. The literature is entirely art—"stateliness" is the characteristic. But Eliot insists that in the work of Shakespeare or Donne, "in" the blank verse or the newly formed prose, is "curious knowledge of the human heart." This is what the art amounts to.

Closely connected to this issue of the "real" in Shakespeare, or "knowledge of the heart," is Eliot's interest in Shakespeare's grasp of the "typical," an interest that begins early for Eliot and continues throughout his career. In the "Massinger" essay, where Massinger's drama of "social abstractions" is set against greater drama of the time, Massinger is said not to achieve "the truly typical," "for the *typical* figure in a drama is always particularized—an individual." This means, Eliot makes clear, that the figure's speech and action have been worked to the point of achieving an actual emotion. He has just explained that when "Massinger's ladies resist temptation they do not appear to undergo any important emotion," for Massinger suffers from a "paltry imagination" (*SE,* pp. 189–90). It is notable that "imagination," the faculty for achieving the work of art, for "intensification" or "transmutation," is declared by Eliot to be the very faculty for giving us the "real" and "typical." The point is very close to that in "Andrew Marvell," where Eliot quotes Coleridge on the at-oneness of the general and the particular in true imagination and where he examines poems of Marvell to show the suggestion of the general in the concrete, even the "trivial" (*SE,* pp. 256–59).

In the second "Marvell" essay, where Eliot comments on the "strong toil of grace" lines from *Antony,* the "inevitability" is said to lie not only in the form of the language, the "fusion" of language and "things," but also in the fact that the words are "appropriate to be spoken by any character."[35] The words particularize a situation—they are suitable to the mood of Octavius in the end—but they also "explain" what anyone must see in the attitude of Cleopatra. It is not just a moment in a drama, it is the final moral exposure— we are in the realm of the most general. In the introduction to Charlotte Eliot's *Savonarola* Eliot remarks, apropos of historical drama, that the heroes of Shakespeare and Corneille are often noted to be always courtiers of the sixteenth or seventeenth century; but, he says, "they are therefore more vital and accordingly truer to the life of any and every time than, for instance, the figures of Sienciewitz" (the author of *Quo Vadis*, d. 1916)—the latter are just "archaeology."[36] Shakespeare has been able to particularize, using the life he saw about him, obtaining "vitality"; this, it seems, is what can be generalized to other historical periods.

In the "Middleton" essay (1927) Eliot says the characters in *The Changeling* are "real" and driven by "fundamental motions" toward good or evil. What we are given is a "dispassionate exposure" of the general motives (*SE*, p. 141). He goes on to speak of "the stratum of truth permanent in human nature" that Middleton exposes, and he compares the tragedy of Beatrice to those of Oedipus and Antony, where a character not unnaturally bad is "caught in the consequences" of his action (p. 142). The "reality" in all these cases would seem to be due to the being driven by "fundamental motions." Further, Eliot says that Middleton with Beatrice has shown us a "process": Beatrice becomes "habituated" to her sin. And such a "process" is the "essence" of *Macbeth*— "habituation to crime" (pp. 142–43). A general "process," in a sense a "fundamental motion," can be seen as the "essence" of a tragedy. (The rest of the "Middleton" essay is a discussion of his other plays in much these same terms, the general human traits Middleton locates and "exposes.")

By the time of the "Middleton" essay, of course, Eliot had already converted to Christianity, and his way of talking here about the general interest of drama—"fundamental motions of humanity to good and evil" and so on— sounds perhaps Johnsonian. Eliot's friends have noted that he felt very close to Johnson around 1930 and later,[37] though Eliot never addressed in his published writings Johnson's own disposition for the general in Shakespeare. Certainly, there is in this work a rather different strain of interest in the general than in Eliot's earlier work. I have remarked on his interest in Frazer and "the vanished mind of which ours is a continuation," also on his connection of Frazer's revelation to the work of various artists—Stravinsky, Joyce. The discussion of the "savage farce" of Marlowe and Ben Jonson, the "terror" in Bishop King (the same that is in Poe), the "scandal" in Shakespeare, all bring this interest to the art of the period of Shakespeare.

But more "civilized" Johnsonian terms are found early in Eliot, as in the "Massinger" essay and "Andrew Marvell," which talk about the general and do not bring up "terror"; while Eliot's interest in the primitive continues on into his later criticism (as in the essay on Djuna Barnes's *Nightwood*, which compares the work, as a picture of abiding "horror and doom," to Elizabethan drama; or as in the 1937 Shakespeare Lectures, which discuss the musical means and mysterious effect of the recognition scenes in the late plays). In the "London Letter" that connects Frazer to Stravinsky, Eliot complains about Shaw: "Had he been more curious about the actual and abiding human being, he might have been less clever and less surprising [this cleverness has offended Eliot]. He was interested in comparatively transient things, in anything that can or should be changed; but he was not interested in, was rather impatient of, the things which always have been and always will be the same." Perhaps the next generation "may find . . . permanence more interesting than change."[38] Is the idea of the permanent here a Johnsonian or a Frazerian one? The answer is probably both. Eliot's interest in the "typical" or "permanent" in human life, and its place in drama and other art, is one interest, I suggest, capable of provisional explanation in either "classical," Christian, or anthropological terms. There is just too much mixing of, and movement among, points of view to suppose otherwise.

It is probably in light of Eliot's developed interest in the "typical" or "permanent" that we ought to understand his comment in the early "Dante" essay on Shakespeare's "critical" approach to his material. Where Dante places the isolated character or emotion in its place in the great range of personages and states of being throughout the poem, "Shakespeare takes a character apparently controlled by a simple emotion, and analyses the character and the emotion itself. The emotion is split up into constituents—and perhaps destroyed in the process. The mind of Shakespeare was one of the most *critical* that has ever existed."[39] This comment is meant first as a *formal* description: the ordering and the whole in Dante is one thing; Shakespeare's pursuit of his one subject until he has finished with it—or it has finished itself—is another. But such a description of Shakespeare indicates a moral interest as well. Shakespeare questions something in human nature in order to expose the ingredients and tendencies we may not have seen.

Eliot uses the term "critical" of works of art in two other senses than we see here, but with every use he has in mind the artist's revelation of something in human nature. In the "Ben Jonson" essay "critical" is distinguished from "creative" satire; the former, as in the work of Molière or *Education sentimentale,* asks the reader continually to make connections to a recognizable (or plausible) world of human beings. Of course, we are told the distinction is only relative; Jonson's work is ultimately critical too, giving us a new point of view from which to inspect the actual world.[40] We might ponder Shakespeare's place, or that of any artist, on the scale from "critical" to "creative." In another sense Eliot uses the term "critical" of the work of a number of novelists—Turgenev, Henry James, Hawthorne—for their habit of creating a "situation," a dramatic internetwork among characters who are thus each understood in light of the others; further, "a civilization is criticized." The same point is made without the use of the term "critical" about Edith Wharton, Wyndham Lewis, Stendahl—they are by implication "critical" too.[41] This weighing of personages and values against one another sounds like the account of Dante, in *contrast* to Shakespeare, that appears in the "Dante" essay. And, of course, Dante is to be appreciated for enforcing the truths of human nature and of life in this world.

Perhaps Eliot designates Shakespeare as "critical" for the poet's persistent study of human nature in the purely human realm (as is the case with the novelists), a persistence that takes form in Shakespeare's case as a certain pursuit, splitting up, and perhaps "destruction" of the play's subject matter, all of which amounts to a certain *kind* of whole. Dante also reveals human nature, but it is by intensifying, making clearer, what a traditional theological philosophy teaches, a philosophy available in terms other than Dante's. Shakespeare, like the novelists, works in a realm where there is constant new discovery and a finding of new terms for things.

Reservations about the Elizabethan Age

The discordant part of Eliot's criticism in the twenties is his voicing of some doubts about Shakespeare and his age—the mentality of the age and the nature of its art. Eliot shows negative feelings about Shakespeare here; but on the whole Eliot excepts him from other writers or just worries about whether to include him within general strictures on the age. This worry is not resolved until the last years of the twenties, when Eliot concentrates on the question of meaning in Shakespeare and then accepts, in the introduction to *The Wheel of Fire,* the notion of a positive vision in Shakespeare. After this point we hear no more discontent with Shakespeare.

"Four Elizabethan Dramatists" (1924) expresses a passion for abstraction and convention in drama that is carried to an extreme Eliot never otherwise goes to. The essay has the air, like the earlier "Hamlet" essay, of being intended to produce a shock, to make us begin thinking in new ways. It appeared in the sixth issue of *The Criterion,* only Eliot's third full-scale article there, with the impressive subtitle, "A Preface."[42] The points of the essay are to interest the reader in Elizabethan drama; to insist that it is at once poetic and dramatic, against Lamb and Swinburne, who merely savored its poetic aspect; and to defend the very idea of a poetic drama against William Archer and the taste for realistic drama of the late nineteenth and early twentieth centuries. Archer, theater critic and playwright, champion of Ibsen and Shaw, was an object of complaint for Eliot back in "The Duchess of Malfi," where he says the bad production of the work plays into Archer's hands.[43] Now, in 1923, Archer had published *The Old Drama and the New,* surveying the Elizabethans— though carefully sidestepping Shakespeare—and making them out as barbarous and ludicrous compared to Ibsen and other moderns.[44] Thus, Eliot is *for* the Elizabethan drama, and at the end of the essay he makes some positive comments on Webster and Chapman, with the promise of more to come.[45]

But in the central part of the essay Eliot concludes that Elizabethan drama opens itself to the criticisms of a critic like Archer because it is not pure enough in its conventionalism; it has an "aim of realism" with no clear limits drawn. *Everyman* is held up as an ideal of "abstraction"; even Shakespeare, it is said, "like all his contemporaries, was aiming in more than one direction" (*SE,* p.

93). Eliot argues that Elizabethan plays, including Shakespeare's, are difficult to perform because no one conventional style can be maintained; the plays themselves are a mixture of more and less realistic styles (pp. 93–97). After complaining a good deal about the dissatisfactions of playgoing, Eliot comes back to the incongruities of the texts themselves, calling it an "error" to have introduced into *Macbeth* ghosts of such different types as the witches and the ghost of Banquo. Eliot may seem to resolve his own difficulty, however, when he notes the "error" to be "condoned by the success of each passage in itself." And he concludes with what can be taken either as a complaint or as a definition of the very success and wonder of this drama: "The aim of the Elizabethans was to attain complete realism without surrendering any of the advantages which as artists they observed in unrealistic conventions" (p. 97). A final thought, before turning to Webster and Chapman, connects the art of the Elizabethans to their general state of mind: the philosophy, the attitude to life, of the period is one of "anarchism," "dissolution," "decay." In their attitude to life and in their art, the Elizabethans are "greedy," unwilling to accept any limit and abide by it (p. 98). In sum, the essay seems to express doubts, almost fears, about what is a basic great admiration for the art concerned. Certainly, Eliot hopes to provoke readers into thinking anew about the art of *Everyman* and the *Everyman*-like aspect of Shakespeare and the Elizabethans.

The central document in Eliot's new thinking on the Elizabethan age is the unpublished Clark Lectures of 1926, which rather avoid the matter of Shakespeare. This work is part of Eliot's growing interest not in Dante—that was always there—but in the culture behind Dante, and surely part of Eliot's whole movement toward accepting the Christian faith, which he did formally in 1927. The lectures are concerned principally with Donne and the metaphysical poetry of the seventeenth century. Eliot proposes a delicate and—typically of him— relative use of the term "metaphysical" for a certain convergence of thought with poetry that occurs in poetry of some ages—occurs, relatively speaking, with regard to the non-"metaphysical" poetry of other ages (Lecture I). Eliot makes comparisons between the seventeenth-century English and other "metaphysical" poetry: Dante and the trecento (Lecture III) and the nineteenth-century French (Lecture VIII, the final lecture). The English Renaissance is made out as newly self-conscious, tending in its poetry to "tease" feeling out of thought, destructive and controversial in its treatment of ideas (Lecture II); while the poetry of the trecento is seen as focused on the object of thought, direct in its wording, helped and guided by a philosophy widely held (Lecture III). Eliot is very fair to Donne (and other metaphysical poets), who receives much extended analysis and high praise. But Donne is said to be, in comparison to Dante or Cavalcanti, less interested in the idea than in the manner of conveying it. Self-consciousness and uncertainty of mind manifest themselves in a quality of "superfluousness" in the use of language (Lecture IV).

Shakespeare is mentioned very little in the lectures. But Eliot does take occasion, in the fourth one on "superfluousness" in language, to say that the "strong toil of grace" lines from *Antony* are "necessary" in a sense beyond Donne—"an image absolutely woven into the fabric of the thought" (Lecture IV, p. 6). Shakespeare is placed with Dante and Catullus, beyond Donne, in the region of "highest" sincerity (p. 17). The lectures as a whole, with their discussion of Renaissance self-consciousness and new "psychology" or psychologism, the question of Descartes, and related matters, would be highly interesting brought into relation to Shakespeare. One has the feeling Eliot does not know quite what to do with Shakespeare here. But he suggests a way to consider the question, in a comment on Racine: In regard to the "teasing" of thought for emotional possibilities, as in Donne, Racine is said to get this sort of "poetic value" (as with Phaedra on not having known Hippolytus earlier in life) while at the same time getting the "dramatic value" of characterization of the individual and placement in the context of action—restoring sanity, as it were, by command of the whole drama (Lecture II, pp. 19–21). Eliot allows in other essays that Shakespeare is to be seen to work in this way.

Discontent with Shakespeare flickers in essays of the next few years. In a review of Root's edition of Chaucer's *Troilus* (1926) Eliot speaks of Chaucer as having arrived, before writing, at the place he was going in thought; Chaucer was thus able to place the characters in his poem in a settled order. Shakespeare's *Troilus,* however, is "the passing fury of a prodigious and for the moment irresponsible Titan, working his way almost blindly through destruction towards his own ends."[46] Not exactly dispraise, but Eliot seems overwhelmed by Elizabethan "anarchy." In "Seneca in Elizabethan Translation" (1927) he comments on the influence of Seneca's plays upon the Elizabethans, saying that the "horrors" go much further in the Elizabethans, Shakespeare included, than in Seneca and that there was in Shakespeare's age "some fundamental release of restraint" (*SE,* pp. 65–68). Later in the essay Eliot says it inspires us with "terror and awe" that Shakespeare was able to base "the greatest poetry" upon a Senecan attitude to life, as in the prison scene with the Duke and Claudio in *Measure for Measure* or in *Lear* generally (pp. 80–81). Again, not exactly dispraise, but a certain puzzlement obtains. The next year, in a review of Baron von Hügel's letters, Eliot says Hügel is right in suggesting that it is "worth pondering" whether Shakespeare is not bound by Renaissance limits, lacking the sense of the supernatural or God, his dying figures unable to look "forward"; is Shakespeare just an explorer of man's middle depths?[47] In the same year, 1928, in a review of Strachey's *Elizabeth and Essex,* Eliot voices agreement with Strachey that "inconsistency and contrast" were admired in the age; that Shakespeare's plays show such inconsistency and contrast; that what we may disapprove of, the Elizabethans were inclined to let "flourish."[48] This may be taken just as description, but certainly Eliot is putting himself at a distance from the Elizabethan age.

Perhaps the best place to conclude this account of Eliot's worries, before he goes on to resolve them in the essays around 1930, is with the "Dialogue on Dramatic Poetry" (1928), whose very form suits an uncertainty on the part of the author. The "Dialogue" was written to be published with its model, the "Dialogue" of Dryden. Dryden, himself a notable Shakespearean, also had doubts enough about Shakespeare to want to "improve" him. The conversation occurs among figures labeled "A" to "G," and Eliot's own thinking cannot be pinned down in any one place. "B" and "E" begin to agree that "Shakespeare fails us" in a certain sense and that William Archer ought to have attacked him with the other Elizabethans. There is missing a "background of social order"; we see only "weakness of character" going to disaster. Shakespeare is not to be isolated from his age, which moved as a whole toward "anarchy and chaos." But "E" comes to think that in fact the Elizabethan drama, certainly Shakespeare, does "justify artistically" the anarchic background. And "A" is provoked to make the following inquisition:

A: . . . Are you prepared to say that you are the worse for having read Shakespeare and seen him played?
B: No.
A: Are you prepared to maintain that you are none the better, none the wiser, and none the happier for it?
B: No . . . I would not suppress anything that is good by artistic standards. For there is always something to be learned from it. I would not have Shakespeare any different from what he is [*SE,* pp. 40–42]

One further note on Eliot's mixed feelings in these years — while he is expressing some doubts about Shakespeare, *The Criterion* is steadily publishing articles and reviews (by Herbert Read, Middleton Murry, and others) that take an unreserved philosophical interest in the plays and accord Shakespeare the highest praise. Except for "Four Elizabethan Dramatists," no negative thoughts about Shakespeare can be found in the pages of *The Criterion.* (See the appendix, which lists and describes the critical or interpretive articles on Shakespeare in *The Criterion* by others than Eliot.)

3

The Problem of Meaning: 1927–37

In the 1920s Eliot developed an elaborate view of the Shakespeare play. He covered the use of language; the nature of the created character; the whole "poetic vision"; and the involving, overpowering effect of the plays for the properly open audience. But Eliot raised doubts about Shakespeare's intellectual coherence, and it is clear that this question is not to be distinguished from that of artistic coherence. Does Shakespeare perhaps fail as an artist because of something unsatisfactory in the intellectual realm?

Eliot's chief Shakespearean interest from "Shakespeare and the Stoicism of Seneca" of 1927 until the Shakespeare Lectures of 1937 is the question of meaning. If the "poetic vision" does not embody a philosophy, if it is only to be described as a "point of view," then just what is that? In the middle and later twenties Eliot addresses the question of poetry and content or belief with regard to literature in general, speaking at length about the case of Shakespeare in "Shakespeare and the Stoicism of Seneca." Poetry makes a difference to whatever thought or life it is involved with. It brings its materials into a "unity," having "informative" value, even being "consoling." In the introduction to *The Wheel of Fire* Eliot goes further, endorsing the idea of a substantive "vision" in Shakespeare, which he continues to discuss in work of the next several years.

Intellectual Coherence

We see a beginning to Eliot's new thoughts on meaning in a 1924 essay on Valéry. In this introduction to a translation of *Le Serpent* by Mark Wardle, Eliot is confronted with a philosophic poem, as much philosophic as poems tend to be; he is called upon to push his thoughts a bit on the nature of philosophy and that of poetry. The essay, like the 1920–21 "Prose and Verse" and "Modern Tendencies in Poetry," is one of Eliot's fullest, most helpful discussions of the transmutation of life and thought into art. Like others, this essay comes down firmly in favor of an "impersonal" achievement that yet takes its beginnings in plenty of personality and "passion."

Eliot says Valéry has recognized that "not our feelings, but the pattern which we may make of our feelings, is the center of value." But he goes on to insist that Valéry is not "an 'intellectual' poet, in contrast to poets of emotion and vivid depiction of life." Eliot will not see in Valéry a "philosophy," a "metaphysical system, over and above his poetical system of organization." "In *La Pythie* I find, not a philosophy, but a poetic statement of a definite and unique state of the soul dispossessed. In *Le Serpent* I do not find a philosophy, but a poem which has existing parallels [the Upanishads are mentioned]. . . . But this theme has never before, and will never again, have *this* expression."[1] There is in the poetry a "pattern," which is not a "philosophy" but a "poetical system or organization." A philosophy may be seen, it is implied, but not "over and above" this system of organization. What the poetry states is the poet's *experience* of a philosophy (so Eliot will put it in the "Dante" essay), where the poet brings philosophical thought, as all the rest of life, to the state of a "pattern" that is a work of art. There is "statement," but of a "state of the soul." There is what can be paralleled in other statements, but it has "*this* expression," making of what can be paralleled something it has never been.

Eliot said in an early essay on Kipling that the work of Shakespeare, Conrad, and others has what should be called a "point of view" rather than a "philosophy." Kipling is something else—"oratorical" about a few common ideas. But in a *Criterion* "Commentary" of 1926 Eliot is more impressed with Kipling's own work, claiming his books are "more than reportage," that they have a "sense," indeed a "meaning."[2] This is not a departure from the term "point of view" but is certainly an emphasis more on the intellectual, or intellectual-like, dimension of a writer's work.

In a 1927 review of Una Ellis-Fermor's book on Marlowe Eliot speaks of *Tamburlaine* as a "vehicle for Marlowe's philosophical speculations." He also admits a "philosophical quality" to the dramatist's mind, but only as long as we are clear that "the value of Marlowe's verse is inseparable from the value of his thought" (with imagery, he is "employing only as exact a vision as is necessary to realize an idea"). We do come to a philosophical mind with Marlowe, insofar as we allow the quality of the verse to shape, so to speak, our understanding of this mind (Eliot offers all this as being in agreement with Ellis-Fermor). Eliot takes the occasion to remark that it is the same, in effect, with Shakespeare: "The value of Shakespeare's verse transcends and includes his thought."[3] This point is not so distant from earlier discussion of metaphor, and the means of poetry in general, as a realization of thought; just as the point about Valéry's giving an unprecedented "expression" to matter that can be "paralleled" is not so far from the discussion in "Andrew Marvell" of the "Coy Mistress" as "renewing" a conventional theme.[4] But thought in the earlier essays was something very local, almost the feeling of a moment, and the conventional theme was a "commonplace," easily paraphrasable. In later essays

Eliot dwells on thought in a larger sense, something that might be taken for "philosophical speculations," and on theme as something more complicated than a traditional commonplace. Art is still art, but it may have, as is said of Kipling's work, a "sense."

"Shakespeare and the Stoicism of Seneca" is the principal work in which Eliot emphatically insists that we must not call poetry, in particular the plays of Shakespeare, philosophy. Yet we must see that literature does something with the ideas involved in it and thus has "informative" value. The essay is Eliot's chief account (at least until he is ready to talk about a positive "vision") of the middleground or borderland between thought and a supposed "meaning-less" art, pure redaction of life or pure fancy. He goes on and on to make certain this delicate point. But the piece was also a public talk. It is witty, and Eliot seems to enjoy the sound of his voice. He says plainly at last that he has the highest estimate of Shakespeare, believing there is "nothing greater." And he says he feels qualified to discuss Shakespeare because he feels very unlike him. Eliot is suspicious of Lytton Strachey, Middleton Murry, and Wyndham Lewis, because their discussions make Shakespeare out to sound like themselves (*SE*, pp. 108–9).

Eliot thinks "a stoical or Senecan Shakespeare is almost certain to be produced" and wishes "to disinfect the Senecan Shakespeare before he appears." Shakespeare did not take a "view of life" from Seneca but used a Senecan view for "theatrical utility," just as he and other Elizabethan dramatists used an idea of Machiavelli "for stage purposes" (pp. 109–10). Thought and attitudes of various sorts are worked into something larger, or different, which is a play. But before Eliot focuses on the question of what becomes of thought or philosophy in a play, what "theatrical utility" or "stage purposes" amount to, he devotes a few pages to this "Senecan attitude" that appears in Elizabethan drama, centering his comments on Othello's last speech as an effort at "cheering himself up." These pages are perhaps Eliot's best known bit of commentary on Shakespeare, and the passage has been highly influential. One can only compare it to Eliot's general provocation to read the poetry of Shakespeare, like any poetry, closely or perhaps to his remarks on whether *Hamlet* fulfills the idea of "objective correlative."[5]

The argument about Othello's speech is familiar. Eliot picks up his idea from "'Rhetoric' and Poetic Drama" about moments when the character "*sees himself* in a dramatic light" (Othello's last lines are one of the examples he gives there); he speaks now of "the attitude of self-dramatization assumed by some of Shakespeare's heroes at moments of tragic intensity." Other Elizabethan writers are noted as showing this attitude as well. Othello's final speech is not to be taken at "face value, as expressing . . . greatness in defeat." Instead, the speaker is "cheering himself up," "endeavoring to escape reality," "thinking about himself" (not Desdemona), "adopting an *aesthetic* rather than a moral attitude, dramatizing himself against his environment." This attitude of self-dramatization is to be seen in the deaths of several other of Shakespeare's protagonists—Coriolanus, Antony, Hamlet; "Hamlet . . . dies fairly well pleased with himself" (the address to Horatio is quoted) (pp. 110–11, 113).

Eliot quotes the speech:

> Soft you; a word or two before you go.
> I have done the state some service, and they know't,—
> No more of that.—I pray you, in your letters,
> When you shall these unlucky deeds relate,
> Speak of me as I am; nothing extenuate,
> Nor set down aught in malice: then must you speak
> Of one that loved not wisely but too well;
> Of one not easily jealous, but, being wrought,
> Perplex'd in the extreme; of one whose hand,
> Like the base Indian, threw a pearl away
> Richer than all his tribe; of one whose subdued eyes,
> Albeit unused to the melting mood,
> Drop tears as fast as the Arabian trees
> Their medicinal gum. Set you down this;
> And say, besides,—that in Aleppo once,
> Where a malignant and a turban'd Turk
> Beat a Venetian and traduced the state,
> I took by the throat the circumcised dog,
> And smote him—thus.

Othello begins, "I have done the state some service, and they know't,— / No more of that." It is the old orator's trick of conjuring something up and then pretending to discount it, here the "doing the state some service." This conjuring up of an idea, we may say, is the first stage of Othello's creating an image of himself.

Othello's "then must you speak" ushers in the series of self-depictions: "one that loved not wisely but too well," "one not easily jealous," and, with the speaker becoming more imagistic and storybook-like, "one . . . like the base Indian" throwing away a pearl and "one" weeping like the Arabian trees dropping their gum. Finally, Othello tells the story of the Turk in Aleppo, identifying himself with the "malignant" Turk who deserves smiting. Eliot may have seized on the desperate quality in Othello's repetition, as it were trying one thing after another, "Of one . . . Of one . . . of one . . . of one." But the attitude of the speaker is called "aesthetic," I believe, chiefly because the images and little stories are so much images and stories. Even the general descriptions—"one that loved not wisely but too well"—have a storybook or summing-up, rather than analytic, quality. To be real self-analysis the phrase would need to be more surprising, more disturbing, like Antony's "the wise gods seel our eyes, / In our own filth drop our clear judgments" (III, xiii, 112–13) (and "one not easily jealous, but, being wrought, / Perplex'd in the extreme" is a little story). Eliot sees Othello's self-descriptions and images—"dramatisings of himself against his environment"—more as images and little stories than anything else, more as form than content. Thus, Eliot concludes, something inside the character presses him to avoid one thing and to project another.

One can consider and reconsider the quality of these final speeches of Shakespeare's characters and the states of mind, or stages of their careers, they seem to imply. There has been discussion in the past, and the discussion goes on, as Eliot would surely have liked. One thing in Eliot's argument has not been taken up by later critics: his point that Shakespeare, in what he is doing here, gets at the "typical" or "permanent" and does so by virtue of being "real." He makes the mood of these final speeches "integral with the human nature of his characters." Compared to other Elizabethan dramatists who employ the Senecan mood, Shakespeare is "less verbal, more real." And Othello's last speech is in being "real," also "typical," an "exposure of human weakness—of universal human weakness," of a "*bovarysme,* the human will to see things as they are not" (pp. 110–11).

Eliot says that Shakespeare "is . . . illustrating, consciously or unconsciously, human nature, not Seneca." And he concedes that Shakespeare and other dramatists may have derived their attunedness to the "Senecan attitude" from observation of life or from any number of literary sources (pp. 111–12). But Eliot does argue that the self-dramatizing mood epitomized in Seneca's plays—those works let us give it a name—particularly suits the historical circumstances of the English Renaissance. Stoicism provided a "refuge" in an "indifferent" or "hostile" world. The "dissolution" and "chaos" of Elizabethan England made appealing any attitude offering something firm, "even if it be only the attitude of 'I am myself alone'" (p. 112). Later in the essay we hear of "Renaissance anarchism" as the motive for the fatalism and turning inward to the self we see so much of in protagonists of the plays (p. 114).

Of course, Eliot has been talking about Renaissance "anarchism" for a few years now; in the contemporary "Seneca in Elizabethan Translation" he suggests the suitability of Senecan "posing" to the Renaissance, in much the same terms as in the "Stoicism of Seneca" essay (*SE,* pp. 55–58). It would be interesting if Eliot had brought these thoughts on Renaissance uncertainty about values, and the need to pose, into connection with his thoughts in the Clark Lectures on Donne's self-consciousness and its relation to Descartes and a new "psychological" preoccupation and tendency to doubt one's senses. But Eliot does not speculate on this larger connection. He does not mention Donne or Descartes in the "Stoicism of Seneca" essay. And he rather avoids Shakespeare in the Clark Lectures, remarking only in passing that the dramatist, even speaking through characters, does not partake of the "superfluousness" of language found in Donne and other "self-conscious" writers.[6]

But whatever the suitability of Senecan "posing" to the Renaissance, and however helpful it may be to designate the "new attitude" as "Senecan," "this individualism . . . was, of course, exploited largely because of its dramatic possibilities" (*SE,* p. 112). "[Shakespeare] *used* all of these things, for dramatic ends" (p. 114). Eliot has said he wishes "to disinfect the Senecan Shakespeare before he appears"; that is, he argues against the idea that Shakespeare's work amounts to a philosophy. Shakespeare does not simply present us with a Senecan view of life, as some have said he presents a Montaignean or a Machiavellian view of life. Wyndham Lewis's *The Lion and the Fox* had just appeared in 1927, arguing that Shakespeare is a "thinker," that he is to be personally identified with his heroes at the great moments of suffering and complaint against life, that the work in its ultimate effect is critical of life itself, of action as such.[7] Eliot sums up Lewis in his own way, as proposing "a Shakespeare who is a *positive* nihilist, an intellectual force *willing* destruction" (*SE*, p. 114). He quotes a paragraph of Lewis where Shakespeare's work is said to represent "explicit processes of the intellect which would have furnished a moral philosopher like Montaigne with the natural material for his essays" (pp. 114–15). With regard to Shakespeare, Eliot says, "it is the general notion of 'thinking' that I would challenge" (p. 115). The real point of "Shakespeare and the Stoicism of Seneca" is to say precisely what "stage purposes" or "dramatic ends" are as opposed to "thinking."

A further word about Wyndham Lewis and Eliot's other adversary in this essay, Middleton Murry: It seems likely Eliot had considerable respect for these critics even as he quarreled with them. *The Lion and the Fox* was reviewed favorably in *The Criterion* in 1927 by Bonamy Dobrée (see appendix, part 2, item 8). Eliot himself reviewed a reprinting of the book in 1937, saying it offered the best criticism ever written on several of the plays; Eliot showed sympathy for Lewis's picture of Shakespeare as detached observer and "sufferer."[8] (Eliot does not mention the book when he comments on Othello's last speech, but he must have had it in mind. Lewis is at his most carried away with this speech, saying: "The overwhelming truth and beauty is the clearest expression of the favor of Shakespeare's heart and mind. Nothing that could ever be said would make us misunderstand what its author meant by it.")[9] Eliot snipes at Middleton Murry's view of Shakespeare as "bringing . . . a new system of yoga" (*SE,* p. 107). But he gave Murry space in *The Criterion* several times to argue his view (see appendix, part 2, items 1, 5, 7). And in 1936 Eliot reviewed Murry's *Shakespeare* favorably, saying it is good because of the critic's uncommon understanding of poetry.[10]

As for the main argument of "Shakespeare and the Stoicism of Seneca," Shakespeare does not "think." He "expresses the emotional equivalent of thought." "To express precise emotion requires as great intellectual power as to express precise thought." Here we are close to the argument in "The Possibility of a Poetic Drama" about the intellectual power needed to achieve the pure "statement" or "presentation" that constitutes poetic drama. What Shakespeare does may involve "intellectual power," but Eliot would reserve the term "thought" for what he has always been unwilling to admit in drama, the practicable idea: Lewis and others "fail to show that [Shakespeare] thought to any purpose; that he had any coherent view of life, or that he recommended any procedure to follow." Thought or a line of thought, for Eliot, is what can be taken up—what in fact is so offered—to change the way we live. When we read Homer, Sophocles, Virgil, Dante, Shakespeare, "we incline to believe we are apprehending something that can be expressed intellectually; for every precise emotion tends towards intellectual formulation" (*SE*, p. 115). Here is that delicate middleground Eliot is trying to describe or point to: the "expression of precise emotion," which is not the same as "intellectual formulation" but is also not radically apart from it. The expression of the poets is one thing, but it "tends towards" something else.

Dante's poetry has behind it Aquinas, but the "flies to wanton boys" speech in *Lear* is just as great poetry as Dante's, because it "expresses in perfect language [a] permanent human impulse." Dante does nothing else. We can "learn" no more from Dante than from Shakespeare; for that we must go to Aquinas and enter into the processes of thought and reaction that such writing asks us to do. Shakespeare and Dante are equally "useful and beneficial in the sense in which poetry is useful and beneficial." Both are "emotionally . . . informative" (pp. 116–17). There, in this adverb and this adjective, is the paradox, the delicate object of Eliot's contemplation, which he will not let us call either one or the other.

Both Dante and Shakespeare start from their "own emotions," Dante from his "railings, his personal spleen . . . his nostalgia," all of which "can . . . be matched out of Shakespeare." Both poets are "occupied with the struggle— which alone constitutes life for a poet—to transmute . . . personal and private agonies into something rich and strange, something universal and impersonal." This impulse of the poet toward the "rich and strange," which is *at the same time* the "universal and impersonal," issues in the fact that the poet "in writing himself, writes his time" (p. 117). The impulse toward the "universal and impersonal" will bring the poet close to historically characteristic and suitable ideas—those of Aquinas, Montaigne, Seneca. What begins in the personality becomes, in the end, the "expression of the emotional equivalent of thought," thought we can connect to the poet's world. Eliot says of Dante and of Aquinas's body of ideas: "[Dante] merely made use of it, or a fusion took place between his initial emotional impulses and a theory, for the purpose of making poetry" (p. 118). Again, we are in a region between an emotional impulse, which might have become purely an expression of emotion, and a "theory." A "fusion" has occurred, and we are left in a borderland where one thing "tends towards" another.

Eliot continues to insist that we will not get from poetry what we may from philosophy or, indeed, from religion. We will not get the practicable idea, the idea that makes a certain *kind* of difference to life: "Poetry is not a substitute for philosophy or theology or religion . . . it has its own function. But as this function is not intellectual but emotional, it cannot be defined adequately in intellectual terms. We can say that it provides 'consolation'; strange consolation, which is provided equally by writers so different as Dante and Shakespeare" (p. 118). The function of poetry is "emotional," but not in the sense of being a pure expression of a poet's emotion that we can focus on; rather, poetry has an emotional function *for us*. It does not provide the practicable idea; it is thus not intellectual. But it makes a difference to or serves our emotional state, so to speak. It provides "consolation," "strange" consolation indeed, which makes a difference, but without the idea or line of thought as such. This view of the function of poetry is the same as the view of drama Eliot developed earlier in the twenties, as stirring its audience, involving them, in short, mattering to them without changing their ongoing lives. Eliot maintains this view of drama and literature in general throughout his career (as in "The Social Function of Poetry," 1945).

Before concluding the "Stoicism of Seneca" essay Eliot muddies the waters of the "belief" question. We are inclined to think about what Dante or any poet believes, what, in the way of belief, their poetry represents. Eliot says that the poet "*qua* poet" would better be thought of as not "believing" at all. "We must make allowance for differences in the emotional quality of believing . . . between persons of different occupation, such as the philosopher and the poet." The work of the poet does not stand in a relation to "belief" in the same way the work of a man of different "occupation" stands to belief. Further, "belief" means something different in every age; the work of one poet may stand in a relation to belief very differently from the work of a poet in another age (Eliot has told us, in considering ritual, that "meaning" is something different from age to age). And even within one age, Donne and Chapman are "incoherent" in their ideas, focusing purely on "poetic effects," while Shakespeare brings himself into more serious relation to the ideas; he "was a much finer instrument for transformations than any of his contemporaries, finer perhaps even than Dante" (pp. 118–19).

Eliot was irritated about the question of belief by I. A. Richards's comment (in 1927) that *The Waste Land* was a poem dissevered from all belief. This quarrel with Richards should perhaps be seen as background to Eliot's whole discussion of Shakespeare and meaning from here through the next few years. Eliot replied to Richards on *The Waste Land* in "A Note on Poetry and Belief," saying poetry, even doubting or desolate poetry, can never be separated from something called belief. Belief goes on and on, having a different meaning in every era; *The Waste Land* is implicated in a stage of belief.[11] Still in 1927 Eliot turns the question around, reviewing Richards's *Science and Poetry* and remarking that the desiderated poetry of the future, quite without belief, is an incomprehensible idea because, in a sense, belief has not been needed for any poetry ever—*Lear, Paradise Lost,* Homer. How do we know what Dante believed or *how* he believed it? It is a question irrelevant to our reading of him.[12] We had better not worry about belief, in any simple sense, in reading poetry. Instead, we should surrender ourselves to the play or poem without thought for our own beliefs or lives. We should not consider the poet as in fact having "belief" or even a "life" that we may bring ours in relation to. We should not look for a practicable idea being communicated to us. We should, instead, surrender ourselves to the "sincerity" that is peculiarly of art,[13] that will stir and "console" us "emotionally," apart from the intellect and on-going activities of life.

Eliot sums up at the end of "Shakespeare and the Stoicism of Seneca": "It has been said that Shakespeare lacks unity; it might I think, be said equally well that it is Shakespeare chiefly that *is* the unity, that unifies so far as they could be unified all the tendencies of a time that certainly lacked unity" (*SE*, p. 119). (This remark is close to Wyndham Lewis's more metaphysical one, that "it is [Shakespeare] and not the time that is a reality.")[14] Shakespeare is the "unity." Eliot does not wish to talk here about the placing of characters in a context of values, the weighing of one tendency against another, though he has said that Shakespeare "exposes weakness" in Othello's last speech. Such discussion of placing characters, and of guiding us to a moral center amid a range of mutually qualifying imperfect attitudes, is more the procedure of Knights, Leavis, and others who have taken note of Eliot.[15] Eliot concludes with an emphasis upon the "unity" simply as the presence or there-ness of all that is involved in Shakespeare. The "unity" is for Eliot not so much to be mapped or thought about but submitted to. We surrender ourselves and take the "consolation" that is offered in presence or there-ness as such, consolation that is not intellectual or directed toward practical life.

Eliot continues this thinking on the middleground of poetry, which "tends towards" the intellectual, in the large "Dante" essay of 1929. This essay on the whole is an attempt to talk about the *Commedia* and the *Vita Nuova* as "poetic" creations rather than a retailing of ideas.[16] Mainly Eliot focuses on particular episodes and examples to help us understand Dante's art and enjoy it *as art*. Throughout the essay Shakespeare is brought up for comparison, declared to be different from Dante in this or that respect, but equally great and, like Dante, coming within the perimeters of art. Shakespeare's language is compared to Dante's, as I have noted, and declared to be more "poetical" but equally "necessary." The individual Shakespeare play is said to be best understood in relation to the whole of the plays, as an episode in Dante needs to be under-stood in relation to the whole of the poem. The point in either case is to take the "feeling" of one work or episode in the context of all the other feelings pre-sented to us (pp. 207, 225). Shakespeare is said to understand "a greater extent and variety of human life than Dante"; while Dante understands "deeper de-grees of degradation and higher degrees of exaltation." The particular "under-standings" of the two poets are the materials and also the effect of their art, which is entirely art, and consummately great art in both cases (pp. 214, 226).

Eliot generalizes about poetry and ideas, again in connection with the "be-lief" question. The use of Shakespeare throughout the essay for purposes of comparison makes what Eliot says about poetry in general seem entirely applicable to Shakespeare as well as to Dante. "Philosophic *belief*" is contrasted to "poetic *assent.*" The "belief attitude" of the reader or audience is said to be different for reading philosophy or reading poetry. One "believes" in the ideas of poetry as one believes in the method of the art, in Dante's case "the physical reality of his journey." One "sees certain beliefs . . . as possible," just as one sees a pictured world, or characters, as possible. In short, one enters into belief *as art,* not as "philosophic belief." Eliot has said in "Shakespeare and the Stoicism of Seneca" that the poet's "private belief becomes a different thing in becoming poetry." Our "belief attitude" is a different thing for poetry than for philosophy; it is this attitude that will bring us into contact with the "different thing" a poet's belief becomes in the work of art (pp. 218–20).

In a long note Eliot states that the existence of literature implies this theory of belief in which there is a distinction of "belief attitude" toward philosophy and toward literature. He sees this view as being close to that of Richards in *Practical Criticism.* But Eliot is still annoyed about Richards's remark on *The Waste Land* that it is severed from all beliefs. So Eliot says that he has only been speaking relatively in this essay, that both the idea of poetry as distinct from ordinary belief, and the idea that poetry expresses belief to be dealt with as belief, are "heresies" if pushed to an extreme. We do accept a "relation" between the poet's "beliefs as a man" and his "beliefs as a poet"; we take it that he "means what he says" in a sense. Eliot himself is more moved by "la sua volontade è nostra pace," he finds more "beauty" in it, than in "Ripeness is all," because the Dante is for him "literally true" in the light of his own "experience" (pp. 229–31). Again, we are in a region where art is art and not another thing, but weighted, we may say, toward the intellectual that is to be dealt with as the intellectual.

In the new preface to *The Sacred Wood* of 1928, following Eliot's formal entry into the Church in 1927, he admits (as he virtually does in the note to the "Dante" essay) that he prefers Dante's poetry to Shakespeare's. "It seems to me to illustrate a saner attitude towards the mystery of life." In making such considerations, "we appear already to be leaving the domain of criticism of 'poetry.' So we cannot stop at any point."[17] The preface to *For Lancelot Andrewes* of the same year announces that Eliot wishes to follow new "lines of development" outward from literature into general questions of values.[18] And the *After Strange Gods* lectures of 1933 declare themselves as going beyond literary criticism, applying moral principles to literature, discussing literature from a certain new—for Eliot—point of view.[19] But Eliot is now careful to say he realizes he is crossing a border; as he puts it in *After Strange Gods,* he is taking up a special concern for the *reader* and the life we live as opposed to concern with the writer or the work in itself.[20] The idea still prevails that literature is not in itself ethics or theology but, so to speak, a borderland, where there is this strange "tendency towards" the idea as such. And, in late essays such as "The Frontiers of Criticism" (1956) and "To Criticize the Critic"

(1961), Eliot still defends literature and literary criticism as a special way of thinking that does not cross the border into ethics and theology.[21]

In several places in 1927–28 Eliot comments on the relation of literature, specifically Shakespeare, to the audience in a way that accords with his new preoccupation with meaning. His comments are an extension of the view already familiar that the work is there to be involved with and not thought about in a wrong way. But Eliot's comments now are affected by his new consciousness of what comes close to a meaning. In an essay on Middleton Murry Eliot says, as he does in "Shakespeare and the Stoicism of Seneca," that Murry falsifies poetry by making it a substitute for philosophy and religion; "Shakespeare would be astonished to read his metamorphosis at Mr. Murry's hands." Eliot quotes Jacques Rivière on Molière and Racine, who claims that the purpose of this drama was "to amuse the better sort."[22] The new preface to *The Sacred Wood* also calls poetry "a superior amusement . . . an amusement *pour distraire les honnêtes gens,*" and does so "not because that is a true definition, but because if you call it anything else you are likely to call it something still more false." It will not do to speak of a "criticism of life," "than which no phrase can sound more frigid to anyone who has felt the full surprise and elevation of a new experience of poetry" (*SW*, pp. viii–ix). Yet, in this same year Eliot was willing, introducing Pound's *Selected Poems,* to call *Hugh Selwyn Mauberley* exactly a "criticism of life" and to defend the poem in those terms.[23] In all this there is an element of reaction against the idea that poetry is *more* than an amusement, while the very term "amusement" suggests a distance and contemplativeness in the audience about what is in a sense, as in Pound's work, a "criticism of life." Eliot now sees the audience of Shakespeare and of French seventeenth-century drama not just as involved in something ritual-like, or living the lives of characters, but as "being amused" in a civilized way, taking a view of the whole, which tends toward a significance or meaning.

But ritual itself now takes on for Eliot a new meaningfulness; and he is concerned to specify the precise degree of meaningfulness in drama as opposed to that of ritual proper. In the introduction to *Savonarola* (1926) he speaks of "a line the termini of which are liturgy and realism" and says the "form" of a drama will be "determined by the point on the line at which a tension between liturgy and realism takes place" (this "point" is for the playwright to find with whatever he has in hand on any given occasion).[24] Drama is not liturgy, which would have a full meaning—liturgy *is* religious affirmation. But drama is to be more meaningful than "realism," which is, presumably, just raw transmission of reality, and is incoherent. Eliot goes on about the value of drama, coming close to his point about "consolation" in "Shakespeare and the Stoicism of Seneca." And it is notable that in the analogy of drama to a religious service meaningfulness is seen to amount to affectingness—the power to "console" is at one with the power to "stimulate": "The play, like a religious service, should be a stimulant to make life more tolerable and augment our ability to live; it should stimulate partly by the action of vocal rhythms on what, in our ignorance, we call the nervous system" (pp. xi–xiii).

Eliot became a communing Christian in 1927, and in the "Dialogue on Dramatic Poetry" (1928) he is further interested to make clear the comparison and the distinction between ritual-like drama and ritual as such. The figure "E" suggests that the "consummation of the drama" is the Mass, and he says the only "dramatic satisfaction" he finds now is in "a High Mass well performed." But "B" rebukes "E" and says that in the Mass one's attention ought to be "on the meaning"; "you have no business to care about the Mass unless you are a believer." There is a "difference in attention" with the Mass (as there is a different "belief attitude" toward philosophy or religion as opposed to poetry). With Mass one is "*participating* . . . supremely conscious of certain realities." Apart from the Mass there is a need for "amusement," "some liturgy less divine, something in respect of which we shall be more spectators and less participants" (*SE,* pp. 35–36). Drama stops short of the full meaning of the Mass and of the Mass's full affectingness—with drama we do not "participate" as with the Mass. Here, as in Eliot's other remarks on "amusement," there is a new emphasis on the distance and contemplativeness of drama's audience. The audience is more focused than it would be with "realism," but it is poised as if to consider a *provisional* meaning, what might be put as a meaning.

Shakespeare's "Vision"

In 1930 Eliot wrote an introduction for Wilson Knight's *The Wheel of Fire,* remarking that Shakespeare has "something to say," a "deeper pattern" below the level of plot and character. This is the "poet's world," a "vision." Eliot approves of Knight's method of "interpretation" as helping to point us toward this ultimate significance, while he insists that no interpretation can fully capture it. He continues to discuss the "vision" in Shakespeare on into the 1930s, saying more about its content and dramatic structure and about the way the personal becomes impersonal in the finished play.

Knight announces in his first chapter, "On the Principles of Shakespearean Interpretation," that "with Shakespeare a purely spiritual atmosphere interpenetrates the action, there is a fusing." Each play is to be regarded as "a visionary whole, close-knit in personification, atmospheric suggestion, and direct poetic-symbolism." We are to "work back through" these three aspects to the "original vision they express."[25] This thinking and approach are not unprecedented. Middleton Murry had suggested something like it in the pages of *The Criterion* (see appendix, part 2, items 1, 5, 7), and Knight said he felt very close to Murry's work in the twenties.[26] Knight also pays tribute to John Masefield's "Shakespeare and Spiritual Life" of 1924;[27] in *The Wheel of Fire* itself he mentions approvingly Colin Still's *Shakespeare's Mystery Play* (1921), as does Eliot in the introduction.[28] Although Knight's approach is not entirely new, Eliot endorses it and begins to speak of Shakespeare in terms something like Knight's in part because Knight's work is so impressive. It is plausible to think of Knight as working something of a conversion on Eliot.

A number of points about Knight's work almost seem calculated to impress Eliot, perhaps to stir him to new thinking. Knight says in his first chapter that "the consciousness that awakens in poetic composition" we are to "enjoy" "when we submit ourselves with utmost passivity to the poet's work" (*WF,* p. 7). His discussions of the plays show an excited involvement with the details of the poetry, just as Eliot had often insisted needed to be the case with the reader of Shakespeare. A sensitive reader like Knight, writing of the plays in detail, was likely to make an impression on Eliot and perhaps convince him of larger points about meaning where earlier "philosophical" critics had failed.

Knight tells us in his memoir of Eliot that Eliot had read and liked the 1929 pamphlet *Myth and Miracle* and offered on the basis of this to recommend *The Wheel of Fire* for publication.[29] *Myth and Miracle* makes a great point of Shakespeare's career being a progress, where the preoccupations of one play or group of plays are extended and resolved, in a sense, in succeeding work.[30] Knight reverts to this point in the first chapter of *The Wheel of Fire,* though that work is only concerned with the tragedies (and does not include *Antony* or *Coriolanus*) (*WF,* p. 15). This interest in Shakespeare's career as a progress was, of course, an old one of Eliot's (expressed recently, as I have noted, in the "Dante" essay). Knight's discussion of Shakespeare in this framework was perhaps likely to impress Eliot with points about meaning and substantive theme. *Myth and Miracle* presses very hard for recognition of *Pericles* as a great work and for recognition of the late plays in general as offering the consummate philosophical resolution to problems explored in the tragedies.[31] *Pericles,* of course, provides the material for Eliot's first Shakespeare poem, "Marina"; from this point on through the 1937 Shakespeare Lectures Eliot shows intense interest in the late plays and defends *Pericles* in particular. Whether Knight moved Eliot to his discovery, or simply played into the hands of what Eliot was discovering on his own, is impossible to say. A final point about a strain in Knight likely to evoke Eliot's sympathy and perhaps lead him to accept new thinking on theme and substance: one of the best essays in *The Wheel of Fire,* "*King Lear* and the Comedy of the Grotesque," dwells on the copresence of comic and tragic moods that Eliot had made a special point about in Shakespeare all through the twenties.[32]

But Knight says later of Eliot's introduction, without being specific, that it is not written "from the standpoint of the essays" in the book and that Eliot engages himself in "complications unnecessary" to what Knight is doing with the plays.[33] Indeed, Eliot discusses Shakespeare's "deeper pattern" and "vision," both here and in subsequent essays, very much in his own terms. He endorses Knight's "interpretation," but he sees it as a compromise, merely a help toward making contact with what cannot be described; Knight, on the other hand, is clearly satisfied with spelling out and naming. Eliot commends Knight's conclusions on the later plays and his account of Shakespeare's development. But Eliot does not connect his own remarks on vision to Knight's important—by his lights—conclusions about intellect versus intuition in *Troilus,* or the message of the Gospels in *Measure for Measure,* or the general theme in Shakespeare of transcendent love versus this-world values of honor and war.[34]

Eliot continues to recommend Knight in the thirties (as, of course, Knight produces more books on Shakespeare), but he does so in the Shakespeare Lectures with decided reservations, finding Knight too intellectually specific, asking of the audience too much positive consciousness.[35] In sum, there are connections between Eliot's thinking and Knight's; certainly, Knight made a great difference to Eliot—here at last was a Shakespeare critic to listen and react to continually. But the question of Eliot's precise debt to Knight is unsolvable. Eliot's view of "vision" and "pattern" in Shakespeare, from 1930 on through the Shakespeare Lectures, has its own integrity and its own terms. I will here give an account of Eliot's view just as he presents it.

In the introduction to Knight's work Eliot first speaks of Shakespeare's "something to say"; then discourses on interpretation, its problems and purpose; and finally comes back to some thoughts on how poetic drama is put together and what, in the end, it is meant to convey to us. Eliot begins by noting what he has said before, that even "philosophical poets" such as Dante and Lucretius are not providing us with a philosophy but with "the emotional and sense equivalent" for a philosophy. But now Eliot goes further, saying that this "emotional" or "sense" version of philosophical material is not simply a "parallel," as it were, in another realm, but that "the poet has something to say which is not even necessarily implicit in the system, something which is also over and above the verbal beauty." This "something to say" is part of "the pattern of the carpet" of the poet, and it can be found in the work of other poets than the "philosophical," primarily in Shakespeare (*WF,* p. xiii). Shakespeare does not have Dante's thoroughgoing system as beginning philosophical material for us to compare his own contribution to; further confusion results because Shakespeare worked in a popular theater with its special demands and because various dramatists seem to have borrowed from each other. Thus, there is more need than there is with Dante or Lucretius to study Shakespeare assiduously to see his "pattern" (pp. xiii–xv).

Eliot has said that the poet's "something to say" goes beyond the beginning philosophical material, also that it stands "over and above the verbal beauty." Again, he stresses that what he is pointing to in Shakespeare is not "a pure element in poetry, the right use of words and cadences, which the real amateur of poetry can wholly isolate to enjoy." "The greatest poetry, like the greatest prose, has a doubleness; the poet is talking to you on two planes at once . . . Shakespeare . . . has this doubleness of speech" (p. xv). There is a plane of "beauty" in "words and cadences" and a plane of "something to say" that is the poet's own, beyond his philosophical material. Eliot spoke earlier, in "Shakespeare and the Stoicism of Seneca," of a middleground in Shakespeare where the "purely" poetic "tends towards" the intellectual. Now he speaks of what is decidedly intellectual, a "something to say" distinct enough from the idea of a "pure" poetry to be thought of as a second plane existing simultaneously with that of the pure element of poetry. And the "something to say" is the poet's own, not equatable with his beginning material.

Although Eliot has not spoken before of the existence of this second plane in Shakespeare, he has said as much about other writers. So it was only natural he came to see Shakespeare this way, perhaps without the inducement of Wilson Knight. In the remarkable fifth of the Clark Lectures, on Donne's long poems (Eliot's favorite Donne at this point), he argues that the poems do not in their full effect present the "structure" of thought they seem to offer initially. Instead, a "doubleness" operates whereby recurring images and other qualities of the poetry lead us to a deeper "preoccupation" on Donne's part than does the ostensible material of ideas. Donne is compared in this "doubleness" to Chapman and to Dostoyevsky; indeed, elsewhere Eliot talks about a "crossing" in Chapman of an ostensible secondhand body of ideas with a deeper substantive "otherworldliness."[36] (Eliot continually speaks of "doubleness" because at any moment he is distinguishing two planes, one from the other; but overall in these discussions he is speaking of three things in poetry: ostensible, secondhand ideas; qualities of poetry as such; and the "deeper" substantive interest of the poet.)

"Interpretation" is helpful, even necessary, Eliot now admits, to bring attention to Shakespeare's "something to say," his deeper interest. But Eliot wants to make clear his reservations about interpretation, his view of it as being in any particular case only provisional. What we have *finally* to deal with in Shakespeare is something no interpretation can put into words, however much it may help to make us alert to and more sensible of that "something." Eliot says he has been sceptical of interpretation, tending in the past "to rely upon his sense of power and accomplishment in language to guide him." This account of himself accords with his predominant view in the 1920s of the proper relation of audience or readers to the play, the way of involvement in the "poetic vision." He says now that too often people are inclined with a poem to want to "discover its meaning" "in order to prove that they enjoy it." Real enjoyment, giving oneself to the "power and accomplishment with language," is missed. "When the meaning assigned is too clearly formulated, then one reader who has grasped *a* meaning of a poem may happen to appreciate it less exactly, enjoy it less intensely, than another person who has the discretion not to inquire too insistently" (*WF*, p. xvi).

Still, there is a compulsion to "interpret," "imperative and fundamental," and worthwhile if the act is understood for what it is. The impulse is comparable to that of interpreting the universe by metaphysics, where we are never satisfied by any metaphysics but go on if we are "curious." And with poetry "to interpret . . . to seek to pounce upon the secret, to elucidate the pattern and pluck out the mystery, of a poet's work" is "necessary," just as the study of philosophy itself is necessary, "the surrendering ourselves, with adequate knowledge of other systems, to some system," or as "falling in love" is necessary, or "making any contract" (p. xvii). We are bound to interpret; Eliot implies, in his account both of philosophy and of literary interpretation, that we move continually toward a reality, though no one interpretation will be adequate to it. Quite properly, we stop with no one critic's interpretation. "There must be . . . in every effort of interpretation, some part which can be accepted and necessarily also some part which other readers can reject." "Reinterpretation of one's own" is the proper response of any reader to the proffered interpretation of any critic (p. xviii).

Here Eliot pauses to say that certain points of Wilson Knight are of the order "which can stand indefinitely for other people," showing that interpretation will yield something "solid and enduring," even while there is the need to go on. Eliot says there is "a good deal" of this order in Knight, but he only mentions certain general things: first, his appreciation of the late plays, accordant with Eliot's own discoveries, for their "recurrences of mood and theme," their "steadfast" "integrity of exploration," and their "mastery of language," "undiminished" from the middle period. (Eliot has seen "papers" of Knight on the late plays, which, Knight tells us, may mean *Myth and Miracle* and may mean an as yet unpublished study of the late plays, "Thaisa," submitted to Faber in 1929.[37] Eliot is ambiguous about the extent of his own rereading and rethinking of these plays in relation to Knight's influence. He says simply that "reading his essays seems to me to have enlarged my understanding.") Second, Eliot commends Knight's general consideration of Shakespeare's work "as a whole," "no longer to single out several plays as the greatest, and mark the others only as apprenticeship or decline" (*WF*, p. xviii).

Eliot's praise of Knight's method—"pursuing his search for the pattern below the level of 'plot' and 'character'" (p. xviii)—leads to some final thoughts on the construction of poetic drama and its ultimate "vision." As we have heard before from Eliot, poetic drama is not simply the "decoration" of a play with poetic language and meter. And he goes on: "The genuine poetic drama must, at its best, observe all the regulations of the plain drama, but will weave them *organically* (to mix a metaphor and to borrow for the occasion a modern word) into a much richer design . . . our first duty as either critics or 'interpreters' . . . must be to try to grasp the whole design, and read *character* and *plot* in the understanding of this subterrene or submarine music" (p. xix). The reference to "the regulations of the plain drama" recalls the criticism of Murry's *Cinnamon and Angelica,* that it is too deliberately poetic, not "held down" by the need to make action and characterization acceptable.

The picture Eliot gives of poetic drama as one thing, "organic," conceived in all its aspects from one central inspiration, is essentially the same as the "poetic vision" idea developed in the twenties. Where Eliot goes further now is in his concept of the central inspiration of the drama as a "design" suitable for "criticism" or "interpretation," what he has already called a "something to say." The figure of speech for this "design," of a "subterrene or submarine music," enforces Eliot's old feeling that what the poet has to say should not be abstracted or translated from his work in its specific form of art; we have just been hearing that we can rest in no one interpretation. Our knowledge of the dramatic poem occurs only *by* and *in* our involvement in art as art. But there *is* a "design" or "something to say," and "interpretation"—never quite valid—helps to heighten our sensitivity to what is really beyond the words of interpretation. Shakespeare is so "rare" because his characters are so "nearly adequate both to the requirements of the real world and to those of the poet's world" (p. xix). The "requirements of the real world" are those of the "plain drama," where the audience makes its just demands and has them satisfied, where the audience's attention is first captured. But Wilson Knight's method of pursuit "below the level of 'plot' and 'character,'" directs us to "the poet's world" and helps us to concentrate our attention there, though the critic cannot *give* us this world.

Eliot next discusses Shakespeare's "vision." Shakespeare has "no design upon the amelioration of our behavior"—this we have been told in all Eliot's discussion of the relation of the audience to the drama. Shakespeare "sets forth his experience and reading of life." His "aim" is "to show us a vision, a dream if you like, which is beyond good and evil in the common sense." Moreover, even in the work of Dante, because it is a great *poem,* "the very Catholic philosophy . . . with its stern judgement of morals, leads us to the same point beyond good and evil as the pattern of Shakespeare" (p. xx). The "something to say" that distinguishes Dante from the system he adopts is, in the end, as in the "design" of Shakespeare, a "vision," where we rest in contemplation with no consideration of the practical aspects of our lives. The end with art is a contemplation of what is *present in art.*

Eliot concludes his introduction by reminding us that there will be "an essential part of error" in any interpretation. He states that "in a work of art, as truly as anywhere, reality exists in and through appearances." Wilson Knight and Colin Still are commended for not making the "error of presenting the work of Shakespeare as a series of mystical treatises in cryptogram"; that is, these critics do not offer a simple translation of a "reality" to be seen in Shakespeare behind or beyond the important realm of appearances—"poetry is poetry, and the surface is as marvellous as the core." Still, there is a "reality," the "vision," the "something to say," to which interpretation—just because it is, if it is good, concerned with "appearances"—can jolt us into being more alert. "The work of Shakespeare is like life itself something to be lived through. If we lived it completely we should need no interpretation; but on our plane of appearances our interpretations themselves are a part of our living" (p. xx). "If we lived it completely," we would be in tune with the "reality." This notion of "living it completely" expresses the same view of the relation of audience to play seen in the twenties essays. Now, when Eliot is more conscious of a "reality," a "something to say" in the appeareances of the play, he admits we will be better in tune with this reality than we might be, if we listen to a critic like Wilson Knight, who makes a conscious assessment of appearances, pointing to what they contain or reveal.

This view of a "reality" or "vision" in Shakespeare is maintained in a number of comments going well into the thirties. Eliot strains in this direction in the "Dialogue," when "B," for all his doubts, does not want to admit under pressure that he is "none the better, none the wiser, and none the happier" for any encounter with Shakespeare. The "Dialogue" concludes by proposing "exaltation" as what we come to in a work of Shakespeare (*SE,* p. 45).

"Poetry and Propaganda" (1930) is one of Eliot's fullest discussions of the problem of meaning in poetry. He is peculiarly sensitive here to the range of types of things poetry is doing with philosophy or belief in the work of different poets and different periods. He says of Shakespeare that "it is a natural tendency to philosophize on Shakespeare just as it is to philosophize on the world itself."

> Only, the philosophy of Shakespeare is quite a different thing from that of Dante [who has been called in the essay a "propagandist," in a sense]; it really has more in common with, let us say, the philosophy of Beethoven. That is to say, those of us who love Beethoven find in his music something that we call its meaning, though we cannot confine it in words; but it is this meaning which fits it in, somehow, to our whole life; which makes it an emotional exercise and discipline, and not merely an appreciation or virtuosity.[38]

There is a meaning, though it is finally not to be "confined in words," as Eliot also insists in the *Wheel of Fire* introduction. The meaning is to be experienced, but it is not nameable—this gives the analogy to music, at least to music with meaning such as Beethoven's. The work being "fitted in" to our lives, being for us an "exercise and discipline," is not to say that the work gives us a practicable idea—which *would* be confinable in words—or makes a difference to the externals of life or even to our professions of belief. It is Eliot's old idea of the work's making a difference within stasis. Only now he makes a different emphasis by admitting the Beethoven-like idea of meaning, a coherence that involves more than just the range of feeling to which we submit ourselves. At the end of the essay Eliot makes it quite clear that the "use" of poetry is not to give us something to fasten on to and live by, but to allow us the sense of something as "possible" while we attend to the work.[39] (Stephen Spender says that Eliot wrote to him in 1931, saying he had been listening a great deal to the Beethoven A-minor quartet on the gramophone, fascinated with the gaiety that seems a reconciliation after suffering.)[40]

Still in 1930, in the "Tourneur" essay, Eliot is more specific about one instance of "vision" in Shakespeare. This essay is in the main an account of the Tourneur play as a consistent whole in which the quality of the characterization, the style of verse, and so on work in accord to suit the dramatist's central purpose and his temperament, much as was said of Ben Jonson in the 1919 essay. Eliot tries to characterize Tourneur's special temperament, as in the remark I noted about "tasteless" transition from tragic to comic "so positive as to be itself a kind of taste." Still in pursuit of Tourneur's temperament and purpose, Eliot speaks of the "cynicism, the loathing and disgust of humanity" in *The Revenger's Tragedy,* emotions that "exceed the object" and make the play and its characters seem "projected from the poet's inner world of nightmare." This "horror of life" is worth being realized, because it is a "phase" of life, even a "mystical experience." And Tourneur's realization is to be compared to *Hamlet* (*SE,* p. 166). Tourneur's play or *Hamlet* "realizes" a "motive," "an important phase in life," "a mystical experience." There is thus an end for us in the play. (The idea of the "death-motive" is remarkably close to Wilson Knight's account of *Hamlet* in *The Wheel of Fire* as a prolonged flirtation on the part of the protagonist with death as a state of mind, a negation of life, a point of view from which to see the life around one.)[41]

In a broadcast talk, "Dryden the Dramatist," of 1931 Eliot says of Shakespeare and some of his contemporaries that the stage action seems "the symbol and shadow of some more serious action in a world of feeling more real than ours," the stage action being something like the "ominously weighted" perceptions in dreams. Chapman is instanced as "depart[ing] too far from the direct stage action into the second world which the visual symbolizes," having in the stage action "only overtones" (where Dryden has "none"). Shakespeare manages a stage action as well as may be and still has the "overtones" of the "more serious action" in another world.[42] We are reminded of Eliot's statement in his *Wheel of Fire* introduction that Shakespeare's characters and action are adequate both to the "real world" and to the "poet's world." Later in the talk Eliot says of Shakespeare and some of his contemporaries that they explore sin and suffering and give us something "more than morals" (pp. 39–41), as the *Wheel of Fire* introduction speaks of the "vision" "beyond good and evil," a matter simply of presence in art.

Also in 1931 Eliot writes in the "Heywood" essay that this writer lacks what does exist in the works of his greater contemporaries: "behind the motions of [the] personages, the shadows of the human world . . . a reality of moral synthesis," a "vision" "to inform the verse," where the artist shows "power to give undefinable unity to the most various material" (*SE,* p. 152). Near the end of this essay Eliot says more of the substance of Shakespeare's "vision"—that Shakespeare provides a moral center. The "ethics" of other dramatists are "intelligible" only as leading up to or deriving from Shakespeare's "fuller revelation." Shakespeare *includes* the satiric mode, for example, and moves beyond it. Heywood at last is said to be shallow, dealing in conventional sentiment only calculated to please the "ordinary playgoer"—"there is no supernatural music from behind the wings" (pp. 157–58). "Supernatural music" here is not something vague and otherworldly. Music is the analogy, as it is in "Poetry and Propaganda," because we are speaking of what is experienced, not to be "confined in words." But the music amounts to a moral perspective, a "fuller revelation," an allowing of moral modes to stand against one another in a settled understanding "beyond" conventional "good and evil."

Eliot begins to use the analogy to music more frequently in his criticism— he will sum up his ideas in "The Music of Poetry," 1942[43]—and, with the incantatory *Ash-Wednesday* and the little Landscape poems of the thirties, he might seem obsessed at this time with sound in poetry. Musical analogy in his criticism usually emphasizes the experienced as opposed to the nameable, but there is always the admission of an as-if intellectual quality that Eliot tries to characterize in each case he discusses. The quality of the experience is sometimes more sensuous and local; sometimes it is a matter of apprehending a pattern or shape. The as-if intellectual quality is sometimes virtually a coming into contact with the supernatural, sometimes simply a perspective beyond any categorizable one, like what Heidegger describes as the position thinking is always in pursuit of.

In the essay on John Ford (1932) Eliot makes clear that the vision or pattern in Shakespeare (and others who have it, not Ford) is at one and the same time a matter of coherence, of personality, and of a tapping into what is universal in human nature. The artist, by beginning in his personal concerns, has access to the universal. The artist's comprehension of himself and of the universal together, a comprehension *realized in* the work of art, is the "informing" vision that gives coherence. This coherence is called "deep," and it would seem that in the very distance from surface events and feelings as they are conventionally understood—what Ford or Heywood or Massinger deals in exclusively—lies the quality of understanding as if "beyond good and evil." The artist begins in himself and becomes able to give coherence to a set of characters and an action by an intimation of the universal that is beyond the conventional.

In "John Ford" Eliot speaks of Shakespeare's development as his very concentration upon the special deeper coherence he has to convey. This coherence is seen to be at any point in Shakespeare's career an issue of personality or temperament. Eliot has already spoken of Shakespeare's development. Lately, he has taken the subject up anew: in the 1929 "Dante" essay, where Eliot stresses the need for each play to be understood in its place in the whole; in the *Wheel of Fire* introduction, where Eliot is glad to have Knight confirm his sense of an intrepidly advancing Shakespeare, needing to be understood whole; and in the "Tourneur" essay, where *Cymbeline* is shockingly asserted to be an advance on *Hamlet*. Like each of Shakespeare's plays, *Cymbeline* "adds something or develops something not explicit in any previous play; it has its place in an orderly sequence" (*SE,* p. 165).

The "Ford" essay reasserts the need to understand the "meaning" of each Shakespeare play in relation to the rest (p. 170). Eliot sees development as a matter of the "inner significance" or "symbolic value" "becom[ing] the stronger and stronger undertone . . . to the end" (p. 172). He speaks of the final plays and Wilson Knight's claim that the recognition scenes have symbolic significance.[44] Eliot points out that fathers and daughters held some "very deep symbolic value" for Shakespeare and that the late girl heroines "share some beauty of which his earlier heroines do not possess the secret" (p. 171). There is a personal aspect to what is symbolized. "The choice both of theme and of dramatic and verse technique in each play seems to be determined increasingly by Shakespeare's state of feeling, by the particular stage of his emotional maturity at the time" (p. 170). Still, what is achieved is not just intense personal coloring or consistent distortion, but "depth and coherence of a number of emotions and feelings," "inner necessity in the feeling" (p. 171).

From this recognition of the symbolic realm, coherence, and personal disposition in Shakespeare (and some others), Eliot goes on to think out the relation of personality to the universal—the attainment of this universality is what amounts in the end to coherence or to a settled understanding of what is involved in the play. In a remark reminiscent of the early twenties discussions of character creation Eliot tells us: "A dramatic poet cannot create characters of the greatest intensity of life unless his personages, in their reciprocal actions and behavior in their story, are somehow dramatizing, but in no obvious form, an action or struggle for harmony in the soul of the poet" (pp. 172–73). "Intensity of life" here is a rather open conception; it may mean that which is able to interest us or, indeed, that which suggests a deep understanding on the part of the poet. Immediately, Eliot makes the extraordinary statement that Ford's *'Tis Pity* is "in this sense . . . 'meaningless'" (p. 173). We have not the "intensity of life" in the play; we do not believe in the originating "action or struggle . . . in the soul of the poet"; the play has not "meaning." "Meaning" is seen to depend on the personal dimension in the poet. Ford's play is compared to *Antony and Cleopatra;* it lacks what is in *Antony* "an overpowering attraction towards each other of two persons" and a "relation, during the course of the play, becom[ing] increasingly serious" (p. 174). Shakespeare's personal struggle issues in the great feeling and interesting progress of his characters and action. And it is said of Ford's play when thus compared to Shakespeare: "*In short* [my emphasis] the play has not the general significance and emotional depth (for the two go together) without which no such action can be justified" (pp. 174–75). Eliot is saying, in effect, that the feeling of Shakespeare's play, which issues from the personal struggle of the poet, *amounts to* "general significance" of a "justifying" nature. It is as if, in the terms of "Poetry and Prop-

aganda," we have something *there* to take an interest in and bring into relation
to our own lives. If it is really achieved art, it will then be "general."

After some detailed discussion of Ford (who is paid some compliments),
Eliot returns to his emphasis on the "universal" in Shakespeare and the greater
Elizabethans. This drama is not seen to offer analysis of the particular society
of the time; even the rise of city families is treated as a "foible of the age"
rather than "a symptom of social decay and change" (p. 178). The Elizabethan
dramatists accepted their age and were able to concentrate in their respective
ways upon "common characteristics" of humanity at all times. "In the work of
Shakespeare as a whole, there is to be read the profoundest and indeed one of
the most somber studies of humanity that has ever been made in poetry; though
it is in fact so comprehensive that we cannot qualify it as a whole as either glad
or sorry" (p. 179). Shakespeare concentrates upon the enduring, and in his profound consideration and "comprehensiveness" he is beyond "good and evil"
(which would correlate to gladness and sorrow). Still, Shakespeare and the
other compelling dramatists—Marlowe, Jonson, Chapman, Middleton, Webster, Tourneur—give "the pattern, or we may say the undertone, of the personal emotion, the personal drama and struggle, which no biography . . . could
give us; which nothing can give us but our experience of the plays themselves."
This "undertone of the personal emotion" is declared to be "the essential," as
opposed to "the superficies," of poetry (p. 180). As in the "Valéry" and
"Dante" essays, the personal struggle that forms itself into a work of art is seen
to amount to a concentration upon the universal.

In the "Ben Jonson" essay Beaumont and Fletcher were said to have produced "poetry of the surface" in a pejorative sense because the work did not
issue from the depths and did not form a whole, as does the "surface" of Jonson. In the "Ford" essay Beaumont and Fletcher, along with Ford, are said to
have produced "poetry of the surface" being made of the "stock of expressions"
originally "produced by" the greater writers. "It is the absence of purpose—if
we may use the word 'purpose' for something more profound than any formulable purpose can be" (p. 180). The pattern or undertone of personal emotion,
depth of feeling, the essential, *purpose*—suddenly, we are there, in the realm
of the universal. And the one thing is not "formulable" outside the work; for
us it is only to be experienced. The situation might suggest, as elsewhere, the
analogy of music.

In the Norton Lectures of 1932–33, *The Use of Poetry and the Use of
Criticism*, Eliot concedes that Shakespeare had a "'philosophic' mind" in the
sense that Keats had. Shakespeare, again, did not expound an explicit
philosophy, as did Dante and Lucretius; nor did Shakespeare or Keats
"theorize" upon their poetic intuitions, as did Wordsworth and Shelley, pushing
such intuitions to the point of abstraction or generalization *within* the poetry.
But Shakespeare and Keats are "philosophic" in having submitted themselves
to their times, its ideas and feelings, and worked through to the coherence—if
we want to call it that—of "the highest use of poetry."[45]

Again, in Eliot's 1934 survey of Shakespeare criticism from Dryden to Coleridge, he wants to use the word "philosophic" to describe Shakespeare. The late eighteenth-century German critics are praised for their concentration upon a "poetic pattern" in Shakespeare, relating personages and action to setting, showing "the philosophical significance of character." "They penetrate to a deeper level than that of the simple moral values attributed to great literature by earlier times . . . an element of 'mystery' is recognized in Shakespeare. That is one of the gifts of the Romantic Movement to Shakespeare criticism, and one for which, with all its excesses, we have reason to be grateful." Coleridge is praised for showing Shakespeare's "philosophic mind" at work in the early poems: " 'Philosophic' is of course not the right word, but . . . you must find another word to put in its place, and the word has not yet been found." There is an inescapable "sense of the profundity of Shakespeare's 'thought,' or of his thinking-in-images."[46]

The Norton Lectures give some further thoughts on what Shakespeare has to convey in the end and how it is done. In the first lecture Eliot speaks of poetry in general, becoming quite eloquent on a point he has made throughout his criticism:

> We have to communicate—if it is communication, for the word may beg the question—an experience which is not an experience in the ordinary sense, for it may only exist, formed out of many personal experiences ordered in some way which may be very different from the way of valuation of practical life, in the expression of it. *If* poetry is a form of "communication," yet that which is to be communicated is the poem itself, and only incidentally the experience and the thought which have gone into it. [*UPUC*, p. 30]

"Experience and thought," where a range of "personal experience" is decisive and forming, become finally what they are only *in* the work; we, the audience, get the experience and thought only *as* the work. Eliot focuses on the question of the "use" of the work. We do not come away asking, "What has been my benefit or profit?" The artist wishes to engage us like a popular entertainer; ideally, he would have society absorb and relish what he has to offer (pp. 31–32).

In the sixth lecture, on Arnold, Eliot denies that Arnold's communication theory, where we get behind Wordsworth's poetry to his "estimable feelings," will work with Shakespeare. "I enjoy Shakespeare's poetry to the full extent of my capacity for enjoying poetry; but I have not the slightest approach to certainty that I share Shakespeare's feelings; nor am I very much concerned to know whether I do or not" (p. 115). What Shakespeare has to "communicate" is the poem itself, where "feelings" have entered the sort of "universal" realm, we may say, peculiar to art—the "philosophic" realm of "the highest use of poetry" notable in Shakespeare and Keats in contrast to others. The next lecture, "The Modern Mind," discusses contemporaries who carry on from Arnold in seeking a philosophy behind, or issuing out of, poetry. Eliot answers them by reverting to his quotation from Jacques Rivière about the seventeenth-century dramatist who would affirm "he wrote 'for the entertainment of decent people'" (p. 128).

In the final Norton Lecture ("Conclusion") Eliot speaks of "meaning" in the too-simple sense as possibly useful to divert one habit of mind of the reader while the poem "does its work upon him" elsewhere—"much as the imaginary burglar is always provided with a bit of nice meat for the house-dog." But many poets will want to dispense with such "meaning" altogether (p. 151). As for Shakespeare, there is a genuine "meaning," again, apprehensible in the whole experience of the work:

> In a play of Shakespeare you get several levels of significance. For the simplest auditors there is the plot, for the more thoughtful the character and conflict of character, for the more literary the words and phrasing, for the more musically sensitive the rhythm, and for auditors of greater sensitiveness and understanding a meaning which reveals itself gradually. And I do not believe that the classification of audience is so clear-cut as this; but rather that the sensitiveness and understanding of every auditor is acted upon by all these elements at once, though in different degrees of consciousness. [p. 153]

The "meaning which reveals itself gradually" is what we come to finally in Shakespeare, highly "consciously" if we are driven by the perfectly natural compulsion to "interpret." But there is no "clear-cut classification" of the audience: our apprehension of the "meaning" is not to be separated from our being "acted upon" by what the play is doing at all levels.

This view of "meaning" as bound up in the interest of the play on several levels accords with Eliot's discussion back in the early twenties of the popular aspect of theater—theater that is at once a boon to the dramatist with his special purpose of a "poetic vision" and, at the same time, the thing *in spite of which* that special purpose takes wing. The only difference now is that Eliot is willing to call the special purpose a "meaning"; he is more sensitive to the substantive or as-if philosophical in the dramatist's purpose.

Further remarks in the last Norton Lecture and in other essays enforce this idea of the special "meaning" that is yet in and of the popular dimensions of the play. Eliot says again, as in the first of the Norton Lectures, that the poet aspires to the status of the popular entertainer, to have what he offers received as the popular interest of a whole society (p. 154). And,

> furthermore, the theater, by the technical exactions which it makes and limitations which it imposes upon the author, by the obligation to keep for a definite length of time the sustained interest of a large and unprepared and not wholly perceptive group of people, by its problems which have constantly to be solved, has enough to keep the poet's *conscious* mind fully occupied . . . If, beyond keeping the interest of a crowd of people for that length of time, the author can make a play which is real poetry, so much the better. [pp. 154–55]

The author would have a society in which his "real poetry"—his "poetic vision," his "meaning"—is popular. But, as Eliot argued about Middleton Murry, the exactions of the popular art in turn help "real poetry" to flourish. "Real poetry," it is implied here, is the work of the *unconscious* mind—a notion Eliot will pursue in "The Three Voices of Poetry" (1953).[47] The exactions of popular theater allow the unconscious mind to work in its place.

Eliot suggests that the *integral* relation of "poetic vision" or "meaning" to the levels of popular interest in the play is this: the poet attains *through* concentration on the popular interest the realization of his essential meaning—drawn from his depths—that makes it something universal. This idea is supported by the concluding remarks of the final Norton Lecture: "Poetry begins, I dare say, with a savage beating a drum in a jungle, and it retains that essential of percussion and rhythm; hyperbolically one might say that the poet is *older* than other human beings." And speaking for the last time of the "use" of poetry: "It may make us from time to time a little more aware of the deeper, unnamed feelings which form the substratum of our being, to which we rarely penetrate; for our lives are mostly a constant evasion of ourselves, and an evasion of the visible and sensible world" (p. 155). If it is theater with which we are concerned, the poet may, by concentrating on the "old" appeal of the popular art, not be conventional, but make the popular appeal "real poetry." He may bring the "deeper" in himself and the "old" and "deep" in the popular appeal into accord with one another. So the poet does not let the audience rest in the conventional, but heightens its "awareness" of the "deep" in what already interests it, breaks down for a time its "evasion."

Other essays maintain this sense of the special purpose of the work, the "real poetry," as being integral with the popular interest. In the "Wilkie Collins" essay of 1927 Eliot speaks of the "high-brow" and the "thriller" interest as being one and the same in the mid-nineteenth-century novel; he deplores the modern separation into the "stereotyped" thriller and the serious novel that lacks something of the melodramatist's art of being "interesting."[48] In the middle of the essay Eliot brings a Collins novel into confrontation with *Oedipus Rex*. He concedes the relative acceptance of improbability in the former for the sake of a thrill, compared to the development of character in the latter, where we feel that character determines a certain end for people even if accidents and events were to proceed differently than they do. But the "frontier" of drama and melodrama is hard to determine. Perhaps great drama has always needed a "melodramatic element," the element of "accident," and the degree of this is not to be measured (*SE*, p. 415). The "higher" purposes of drama—concentration on character or whatever else—*partake of* the melodramatic, the accident, the thrill. These things are fundamentally "interesting."

Also in 1927, in "Seneca in Elizabethan Translation," Eliot declares that *The Spanish Tragedy, Hamlet, Macbeth, Othello,* and *Oedipus,* are all inspired by a " 'thriller' interest" centered about "plot" "suspense," and "surprise" (in a sense unknown to Seneca, who is an artist of "verbal effects" and "embellishments," giving his audience entirely familiar story material) (*SE,* pp. 65–66). In the thirties, in "Audiences, Producers, Plays, Poets," Eliot says that a play must first be "interesting" and "exciting"; the audience does not "rally round a theory." And the "interest" of the play must be "one interest throughout"; there is no alternation of, as it were, distinct teasing matter and "higher" interest.[49] In a broadcast talk of 1936, "The Need for Poetic Drama," Eliot says the plot is there to hold our attention, to keep us asking what will happen next. The plot should not be separated from the "whole pattern"—the dramatic poetry must be entirely "relevant" to the plot, while it is also suitable for "study" to discern "depths."[50]

In "Audiences, Producers . . ." and "The Need for Poetic Drama" Eliot picks up his musical analogy for apprehension of meaning (from the *Wheel of Fire* introduction and "Poetry and Propaganda"), and he speaks of the "musical pattern" of a play, an idea he will bring home to Shakespeare in the 1937 Shakespeare Lectures. In "Audiences, Producers . . . ," where he says the interests of a play must come together as "one," he refers to "dramatic form"— structure and appeal to an audience's interest in plot, in the conventional sense of these ideas—and to *"musical pattern"* (Eliot's emphasis)—the presentation of "meaning" beyond the level of plot. "The two forms must be one." Moreover, "musical pattern" is "obtained only by verse"; we are reminded of the centrality of poetry to the whole "interest" of a poetic drama.[51]

In "The Need for Poetic Drama" Eliot recalls his point of the twenties that we are not to think of verse "as something *added* to a play," that "a true verse play . . . is *conceived* and carried out in terms of verse" (my emphasis). The dramatist works "like a musician," "to see the thing as a whole musical pattern." The plot is there to hold our attention. "But underneath the action . . . there should be a musical pattern which intensifies our excitement by reinforcing it with feeling from a deeper and less articulate level." "Intensifies," "reinforcing"—the musical pattern is the same as plot or action, a carrying of action into the realm of meaning; two levels are distinguished only for the purpose of discussion. And that it is "meaning" Eliot has in mind, not an experience indistinguishable from music, he goes on to make clear. "Everybody knows that there are things that can be said in music that cannot be said in speech. And there are things that can be said in poetic drama that cannot be said in either music or ordinary speech."[52] Poetic drama is not declared to be, in effect, music; music is only drawn on as an analogy to caution us against fixation on the paraphrasable. "Things to be said" "that cannot be said in music" is what we come to in the end with poetic drama, if only we come through the formation of art. In 1937, in his essay on Djuna Barnes's *Nightwood,* Eliot praises the book for its "rhythm," "musical pattern," and "raising" of its "matter" to "the first intensity." The characters are interesting by virtue of the "whole pattern," which gives a sense of the human misery and bondage seen in the work as being "universal" and makes of the work something "profound." In sum, the book is likened to Elizabethan tragedy.[53]

Comedy and Tragedy

Eliot continues during the thirties, as before, to discuss the copresence of comedy and tragedy in Shakespeare. But now he has a new emphasis on the way this copresence contributes to the substantive meaning or vision he has begun to talk about.

In the 1931 Dryden talks (which become the little book of 1932) Eliot speaks of Dryden's critical interest in the unities of time and place, to which Eliot is sympathetic, as contributing to "unity of poetic feeling"—Eliot's term. Regarding this "unity of poetic feeling" Eliot remarks, much in the terms he used before, that the Elizabethans, especially Shakespeare, offer the comic as an "intensification of the sombreness" in the plays. The Porter in *Macbeth*, the Gravediggers in *Hamlet*, the Fool in *Lear*, and Lepidus drunk in *Antony* are instanced and said to "make the horror or tragedy more real by transposing it for a moment from the sublime to the common."[54] The "intensification," occurring within the "unity," amounts to a "making more real" of one moment by another—rereading, as it were, one moment through another. With this "reality" we are already coming to something substantive.

But Eliot should not be misunderstood to be talking of "realism," as if he were saying the tragic is a recognizable bit of life made even more recognizable by re-viewing in a comic or "common" light. In the "Heywood" essay (also 1931) he faults Heywood for lacking "imaginative humor" and contrasts *The Witch of Edmonton* with its figure of Cuddie Banks and his dog. Cuddie, "loving the dog whom he knows to be a devil, but loving him as dog while reproving him as devil," is "worthy" of Shakespeare—"[Cuddie] is not 'realistic,' he is true" (*SE*, p. 155). The comic-tragic brings us not to the recognizable, but to what we *now accept* as the "real," the "true." This idea must involve the old one of the thoroughly created, whether that be the "object" of a line of verse, the character in a "firm outline," or the "poetic vision" itself. It also involves the idea of the "universal," what the dramatist's detail enters into, the larger consideration by which he makes that detail interesting to us.

In the second of the Norton Lectures, on Sidney and Renaissance criticism, Eliot makes it clear that the "unity of poetic feeling," within which the comic and serious occur in the best plays, is virtually equivalent to meaning. As he does with Dryden, Eliot sympathizes with Sidney's disposition for "unity of feeling"; he proposes that drama approached this more often after Sidney's time by the natural process of a "maturing civilization." Shakespeare may have started with "comic relief" as a "practical necessity" of the popular theater; what is "really interesting" is what he "made" of the necessity. As we read the first part of *Henry IV* we may want to linger over the Falstaff episodes and neglect the rest. But

that is an error. As we read from Part I to Part II and see Falstaff, not merely gluttonising and playing pranks indifferent to affairs of State, but leading his band of conscripts and con-

versing with local magistrates, we find that the relief has become serious contrast, and that
political satire issues from it. In *Henry V* the two elements are still more fused; so that we
have not merely a chronicle of kings and queens, but a universal comedy in which all the
actors take part in one event.

In some of the sophisticated comedies what had been crude "comic relief" is
more nearly "taken up into a higher unity of feeling." "In *Twelfth Night* and *A
Midsummer Night's Dream* the farcical element is an essential to a pattern more
complex and elaborate than any constructed by a dramatist before or since."
The Knocking on the Gate scene in *Macbeth* is mentioned again, as is the Pompey's Galley scene in *Antony:*

> This scene is not only in itself a prodigious piece of political satire—
>
> 'A beares the third part of the world, man . . .
>
> but is a key to everything that precedes and follows. [*UPUC,* pp. 42–43]

The copresence of comic and serious amounts to "serious contrast," "satire," "a
universal comedy," "a pattern . . . complex and elaborate," a "key" to the
whole work.

Eliot goes on to speak in this lecture, as he is doing more and more, of
Shakespeare's development, giving it here a definition in relation to comic and
tragic moods: "For me the violence of contrast between the tragic and the
comic, the sublime and the bathetic, in the plays of Shakespeare, disappears in
his maturing work." Comparison of *The Merchant of Venice, Hamlet,* and *The
Tempest,* Eliot hopes, will lead others to the same conclusion. A unity of
moods without violent contrast is what becomes more evident. And Shakespeare's work is to be taken as a whole—contrast and combination operates on
this large scale. There are "partial failures," with no "derogation" implied in
the term—"attempts with certain material, leaving more to be said, or a resolution to come" (p. 44). Eliot has said in the "Heywood" essay that "satire" is
only a part of Shakespeare, allowed to flourish in *Troilus* and certain other
plays, put in its place, so to speak, by further work. The notion of meaning
goes beyond the copresence of moods in the one work to the copresence of all
that is in the plays as a whole.

The most interesting point of Eliot's 1934 survey of early Shakespeare
criticism is his praise of Dr. Johnson for finding the traditional division of the
plays into comedy, tragedy, and history essentially incomprehensible and for
preferring, if with some confusion, the comic scenes to the tragic. In his objection to the categorization, "Johnson perceived, though not explicitly, that the
distinctions of tragic and comic are superficial." In his comments on tragedy
with comic scenes, where the latter are preferred, "Johnson is quite aware that
the alternation of 'tragic' and 'comic' is something more than an alternation; he
perceives that something different and new is produced. 'The interchanges of

mingled scenes seldom fail to produce the intended vicissitudes of passion.'
'Through all these denominations of the drama Shakespeare's mode of compo-
sition is the same' " (Eliot's emphasis). As for Johnson's preference:

> Here, it seems to me, Johnson, by his simple integrity, in being wrong has happened upon
> some truth much deeper than he knew. For to those who have experienced the full horror of
> life, tragedy is still inadequate . . . In the end, horror and laughter may be one—only when
> horror and laughter have become as horrible and laughable as they can be; and . . . you may
> laugh or shudder over *Oedipus* or *Hamlet* or *King Lear*—or both at once . . . The distinction
> between the tragic and the comic is an account of the way in which we try to live; when we
> get below it, as in *King Lear,* we have an account of the way in which we do live.[55]

Shakespeare is doing one thing in the comic and tragic or coming to one thing
through the use of both. What we as audience see is a "deep truth," that "horror
and laughter" are "one," Shakespeare's "something to say," that this is where
we really "live."

Eliot's comments on the comic and tragic are related to those on Shakespeare's songs. In the first Dryden talk, reverting for a moment to the
Elizabethan lyric, Eliot tells us that the songs of Shakespeare gain much of
their effect by the "dramatic position." "A song like 'Full fathom five' is suf-
fused by the meaning and feeling of the passage in which it occurs; the songs
of Shakespeare are not interludes or interruptions, but part of the structure of
the plays in which they occur."[56] And it is said in the second Norton Lecture,
"the real superiority of Shakespeare's songs over Campion's is not to be found,
so to speak, internally, but in their setting"; the songs have "intense dramatic
value" by virtue of their place of occurrence (*UPUC,* p. 39). Whether the song
is comic or somber, there is "suffusion" of the setting over the song (and,
surely, of the song over the setting), so that both go to make the one "structure"
of the play.

The copresence of the comic and the serious, and the implication of this
as "meaning," is stressed again by Eliot in a comment on the Shakespeare
songs in his introduction for *Selected Poems* of Marianne Moore. He brings up
the songs as a counterexample when he is complaining that in much "modern-
ist" verse there is too much emphasis either on words or on things; Shakespeare's songs are a model of "fitness" of form and matter. And out of the fitness issues, even apart from a consideration of setting, a convergence of moods
and an implication in meaning. Shakespeare's songs have a "solemnity" by virtue of form itself, however "light and gay" the matter, and a "gaiety" by virtue
of the form, however "serious or tragic" the matter. Shakespeare's songs or
Sophocles' choruses—it is suggested they also have this gaiety with solemnity—"are spectators" of the human action, and they have a "concern besides
the human action."[57] The convergence of moods amounts to a point of view of
height or beyondness in regard to the human action, a "something to say" about
human action from this perspective, as elsewhere the convergence amounts to
a presentation of the "deep" level at which we really live.

The Use of Language

Eliot's comments on Shakespeare's poetry in the late twenties and the thirties seem directed, as they do at all periods, toward keeping our attention on the poetry and reminding us how much goes on in it. But at this time Eliot speaks more often of the at-oneness of poetry and drama in the plays. And he makes the suggestion that dramatic poetry is calculated to convey just the kind of larger meaning, vision, or "something to say" he is talking about so much in these years.

In "Seneca in Elizabethan Translation" (1927) we are told that Seneca's drama is a drama of verbal effects, while

> behind the dialogue of Greek drama we are always conscious of a concrete visual actuality, and behind that of a specific emotional actuality. Behind the drama of words is the drama of action, the timbre of voice and voice, the uplifted hand or tense muscle, and the particular emotion. The spoken play, the words which we read, are symbols, a shorthand, and often, as in the best of Shakespeare, a very abbreviated shorthand indeed, for the acted and felt play, which is always the real thing. The phrase, beautiful as it may be, stands for a greater beauty still. [*SE,* pp. 53–54]

In Shakespeare and the work of the Greeks there is a "real" drama in the words, which is not just words.

In the "Dialogue on Dramatic Poetry," figure "A" early on makes a proposal, which sits well with the others, that verse is no "restriction" on drama, that it amounts to an insisting upon "fundamentals" instead of the mere "appearances" that are the concern of "realism." And "fundamentals" are the "permanent": "Has human feeling altered much from Aeschylus to ourselves? I maintain the contrary . . . The human soul, in intense emotion, strives to express itself in verse . . . feeling and rhythm are related . . . if we want to get at the permanent and universal we tend to express ourselves in verse" (*SE,* 34). A little later, after some discussion of William Archer's mistake in wanting to exclude "poetic" from "dramatic" considerations, "B" proposes that dramatic and poetic "ability" are not entirely different and that "dramatic defects *can* be compensated by poetic excellence." "D" steps in to correct this line of thought, insisting that in great poetic drama the poetic and the dramatic are one and the same. His clarification is not challenged:

> B. makes a mechanical reunion . . . Shakespeare . . . writes his finest poetry in his most dramatic scenes . . . what makes it most dramatic is what makes it most poetic. No one ever points to certain plays of Shakespeare as being the most poetic, and to *other* plays as being the most dramatic. The same plays are the most poetic and the most dramatic, and this is not by a concurrence of two activities, but by the full expansion of one and the same activity. [p. 39]

The "one activity" which is "expanded" in the poetic and the dramatic is "the human soul striving to express itself." Poetry as a form gives us the "permanent," "fundamentals."

In the talk "Dryden the Dramatist" Eliot makes a comparison of *Antony and Cleopatra* with Dryden's *All for Love* and discusses the poetic and the dramatic in general. He pronounces the problem of distinguishing the poetic and dramatic "a tangle," but offers provisionally that "*theatrically dramatic* value in verse exists when the speech has its equivalent in, or can be projected by, the action and gesture and expression of the actor; *poetic* dramatic value is something dramatic in essence which can only be expressed by the word and by the reception of the word." "Expressed by the word," but still "dramatic in essence." Shakespeare is said to have made "the utmost use" of both "values." But Eliot goes on to show by an example that something is happening that cannot be pinned to either notion of value. He compares the words of Dryden's Charmian when the soldiers burst in after Cleopatra's death—"Yes, 'tis well done, and like a Queen, the last / Of her great race. I follow to her. (*Sinks down and dies*)"—and Shakespeare's Charmian—"It is well done, and fitting for a princess / Descended of so many royal kings. / Ah, soldier! (*dies*)." The Dryden lines cannot be said to be less *poetic,* or less *dramatic,* than Shakespeare's (Eliot's emphasis)—"a great actress could make just as much, I believe, of [the lines] of Dryden as those of Shakespeare." But Shakespeare's "remarkable" "Ah, soldier" makes the "difference." You cannot say there is "anything peculiarly *poetic*" about the two words; nor, "*if you isolate the dramatic from the poetic*" (my emphasis), can you say there is "anything peculiarly dramatic" about them—"there is nothing in them for the actress to express in action." What we do have is "a flight above, at which poetry and drama become one thing." Eliot goes on to speak, as noted, of the feeling that the dramatic action is "symbol and shadow" of another action in another world, this immediate one being "ominously weighted" like the perceptions in dreams.[58] Thus, as in the "Dialogue on Dramatic Poetry," the poetry and the drama are seen to be one thing, neither value differentiable from the whole; and this one thing, by virtue of its quality of a "flight above," brings us to the settled perspective as if from another world. This is what the "Dialogue" calls the "permanent" or "fundamentals" and what Eliot overall in these years means by "meaning."

In the final Norton Lecture and in the "Milton" essay of 1936 Eliot comes back to the particularity of Shakespeare's poetry. The lecture says of Coleridge's *Kubla Khan:* "The imagery of that fragment, certainly, whatever its origins in Coleridge's reading, sank to the depths of Coleridge's feeling, was saturated, transformed there—'those are pearls that were his eyes'—and brought up into daylight again." But there is a defect of "organization." The transformed imagery is not fully "*used*" (Eliot's emphasis). Shakespeare is praised for organization, and this lecture gives an account of Shakespeare's "meaning" conveyed by the working of so many levels at once. But Shakespeare is noted by the way to have the same local virtue as Coleridge, to achieve the same "transformation" in detail as his own song from *The Tempest* is used to indicate: "The re-creation of word and image . . . happens almost incessantly with Shakespeare. Again and again, in his use of a word, he will give a new meaning or extract a latent one; again and again the right imagery, saturated while it lay in the depths of Shakespeare's memory, will rise like Anadyomene from the sea" [*UPUC*, pp. 146–47).

The 1936 "Milton" essay underscores the unity of Eliot's criticism. In the essay's attention to detail in Shakespeare, in its criticism of Milton, and in its point of the proper at-oneness of poetic qualities and content or thought it might have been written in 1921 or so. Milton is said to lack "visual imagination," and Shakespeare is offered as a counterexample. The "temple-haunting martlet" speech from *Macbeth* is quoted, as are the lines, "Light thickens, and the crow / Makes wings to the rooky wood." All these lines "not only offer something to the eye, but, so to speak, to the common sense. I mean that they convey the feeling of being in a particular place at a particular time." A further point, similar to one in the last of the Norton Lectures, on Shakespeare's "giving new meaning" to a word: "With Shakespeare, far more than with any other poet in English, the combinations of words offer perpetual novelty; they enlarge the meaning of the individual words joined: thus 'procreant cradle,' 'rooky wood.'"[59]

Later in the essay the syntax of a speech in *Paradise Lost* is found to be "determined by the musical significance, by the auditory imagination" solely, to the diminishment of interest (thus, "musical significance" is on its own not necessarily a value to be approved; "music" in poetry is approved when spoken of as an analogy for a more complex occurrence than music itself). In Shakespeare "the auditory imagination and the imagination of the other senses are more nearly fused [than in Milton], and fused together with the thought" (p. 161). This point sounds like Eliot's old one of poetry as—properly—the realization of thought rather locally conceived. But near the end of this essay he makes clear that he also has in mind his interest in larger, deeper significance. Eliot finds he needs to read *Paradise Lost* with different attention for the "sound," the pleasure of the verse, and for the sequence of ideas.

> Now Shakespeare, or Dante, will bear innumerable readings, but at each reading all the elements of appreciation can be present. There is no interruption between the surface that these poets present to you and the core. While, therefore, I cannot pretend to have penetrated to any "secret" of these poets, I feel that such appreciation of their work as I am capable of points in the right direction. [p. 163]

Attention to the "surface" with Shakespeare—such as Eliot has shown with the lines from Macbeth—has us already involved with the "core" of the work, the "secret." We move toward the core in a "direction" which every fresh reading of the surface will confirm or adjust, letting us go further along.

In connection with this idea of the importance of the poetry in its detail throughout Shakespeare, note that L. C. Knights becomes in the thirties *The Criterion*'s most frequent writer on Shakespeare. In numerous articles and book reviews Knights insists that in the study of Shakespeare we must, above all else, be sensitive and responsive in our close attention to his poetry. (See appendix, part 1, item 22 and subsequent items; part 2, item 19 and subsequent ones.)

"Marina" and *Coriolan* and Eliot's Other Poetry

Eliot writes "Marina" and *Coriolan* in 1930–31, and the poems indicate what his criticism shows: a new acceptance of a coherent meaning in Shakespeare. Shakespeare is suitable now to be recast or meditated upon on the scale of a whole poem. "Marina" is one of Eliot's most delicate poems, complex in its crossings of feeling, unparaphrasable, in these respects like its contemporary *Ash-Wednesday*. Discussions of the poem have always focused, certainly rightly, on the doubleness of experience evoked—this-worldly and other-worldly, death and rebirth, the physical and the transcendent, events in a life and the larger event of a greater life, the building of a boat and the creation of a work of art.[60] Wilson Knight speculates in his memoir of Eliot that the poet was inspired in writing this poem by Knight's own reading of *Pericles* in *Myth and Miracle* and perhaps in "Thaisa."[61] Certainly, the poem may be seen as a restatement or reinforcing of Shakespeare's meaning in the recognition scene of the play, as Knight interprets such a scene: a human encounter that permits access to a transcendent and deathless realm.[62] In judging how much of Eliot's inspiration we can attribute to Knight, note that Eliot says in the *Wheel of Fire* introduction that he was already reading and thinking about the late plays when Knight's work came into his hands. Also, Knight's account of the recognition scene as a crossing of levels of experience is very much what Eliot himself will outline in the 1937 Shakespeare Lectures, though without Knight's emphasis on "love," which indeed the poem does not emphasize either. If one is interested in the play and moved by it at all, it seems almost inevitable to read the recognition scene, with its ceremonious rhythm and Pericles' hearkening to "the music of the spheres," as a crossing of kinds of experience. Perhaps it is best to think of Knight's reading as one thing, Eliot's restatement of the Shakespeare in his poem as another, and the reading of the 1937 lectures as another still. All are notable for their intense interest in the play and their perception of significance within or beyond the immediate.[63]

Coriolan may be taken as actual criticism of Shakespeare's *Coriolanus,* a statement of what the play is about different from any previously offered. Or rather, the poem may be taken this way insofar as any poem may be taken as literary criticism—a complex question into which there is not room to enter fully here. We recall Eliot's repeated insistence that philosophy, or discursive thinking where ideas are offered to be taken up and used, is one thing, and poetry is another. Perhaps *Coriolan* should only be regarded as a recasting of certain traditional material for Eliot's own purposes with, of course, a reaction to current political trends and discussion. Wilson Knight tells us that Eliot asked to see his *Coriolanus* essay (to be published in *The Imperial Theme*) while working on the poem. But Knight admits that what Eliot presents in the poem is not like Knight's account, which describes the play as a contest of the values of "honor" as self-isolating and "temporal" and "love" as communal and finally transcendent.[64] Nor is Eliot's poem much like the account of *Coriolanus* in Lewis's *The Lion and the Fox* (1927), which Eliot had taken an interest in and which he praises very much in a later review. Lewis thinks highly of the play and sees the Shakespeare passion in identification with the godlike figure who must die; but he finds the character "unattractive" and the play in the main a study of this unattractive man in his dealings with his impossible society.[65]

Eliot's poem is more positive about the hero than are Knight and Lewis. The poem's first part, "Triumphal March," presents the man as godlike, poised, having inner depths amid the setting of the parade and the populace, however much there may be a suggestion of disturbance or unhappiness:

> There is no interrogation in his eyes
> Or in the hands, quiet over the horse's neck,
> And the eyes . . .
> O hidden under the dove's wing, hidden in the turtle's breast . . .
> At the still point of the turning world. O hidden. [my ellipses][66]

The second part of the poem, "Difficulties of a Statesman," presents the thinking man dealing with public affairs, impelled to "cry" out, reaching for a union with his mother. (Is she his mother in the flesh or something like the Lady of *Ash-Wednesday*?) The postulated reunion with the mother has an otherworldly aspect: "O hidden under the . . . Hidden under the . . . / Where the dove's foot rested and locked for a moment" (Eliot's ellipses, *CPP*, p. 88). And the poem ends with the double-edged "Resign   Resign   Resign" (p. 89)—is it a turning away from the world or a consolation in this world in light of the otherworldly intimation of the "mother" passage? Eliot's poem may be taken as an affirmation of the positively impressive, deep, even supernaturally sensitive nature of Shakespeare's protagonist, for all his demeanor of sadness—a view that certainly would have been unprecedented at the time of the poem.

Of course, Eliot's poetry is full of references to Shakespeare, from the earliest stage on. Standard accounts of Eliot's poetry mention scores of direct and indirect allusions to Shakespeare, who is brought up in connection with every major poem and with many of the very short ones.[67] There have been numerous articles on the treatment or reworking of Shakespeare in this or that poem, chiefly in those before 1930. "Prufrock" has been noted to recall *Hamlet* and *Richard II* in various ways.[68] "Gerontion" has been linked to Jacques's reference to Touchstone as having a "dry brain" (*As You Like It*, II, vii).[69] *The Hollow Men* has been connected to *Julius Caesar*, both in the theme of boggled "intention" early in the play and in the theme of decayed love between Brutus and Cassius later.[70] And most attention of all has been given to *The Waste Land*—Eliot's setting the poem's material, in "A Game of Chess" and elsewhere, against the grandeur of *Antony and Cleopatra;* the invocation of *The Tempest* in the figure of Ferdinand in "The Fire Sermon" and, of course, in the use of Ariel's transformation song; and other minor references to *The Tempest* and other plays.[71] Ronald Tamplin proposed in an article in 1967 that the whole of *The Waste Land* is structured on Colin Still's reading of *The Tempest* as an allegory of initiation into mysteries, on the model of Eleusis, with barking dogs and so on.[72] James Torrens writes in two articles of Eliot's use of Shakespeare throughout the poetry (still chiefly before 1930). He considers Eliot drawn to Shakespeare's continuing subject of the ambiguities of sex and notes the general diminishment of Shakespearean personages in Eliot's poetry.[73] A Ph.D. dissertation by Gary H. Wilson on Shakespeare in Eliot's poetry is concerned with detail, local evocations and distortions, chiefly in *The Waste Land*.[74] As for Eliot's later poetry, *Ash-Wednesday* begins by quoting the sonnets somewhat askew—"Desiring this man's gift and that man's scope." Grover Smith finds that *The Family Reunion* may be taken as a version of *Hamlet*, as does A. D. Moody later.[75] Moody sees something of Colin Still and initiation rites in "Burnt Norton" (Moody, pp. 241–42). And Smith sees in "East Coker" Falstaff's rising chill of death, Macbeth's notion of "life's fitful fever," and the Theater scene of *Richard II* being changed (Smith, pp. 272–75). The ghost and the preoccupation with historical figures of "Little Gidding" has suggested *Hamlet* to several readers (e.g., Smith, pp. 290, 293).

Even if we accept a poem as "criticism," that is, as representing a view of other literary work that the poet might maintain in either discursive prose or conversation (or even if we accept the poem as "criticism" that could never be translated into another medium), still it is difficult to identify an attitude to Shakespeare's plays in or among most of Eliot's poems. "Marina" and *Coriolan* may not be "criticism," but they begin by seizing a significance in Shakespeare and develop a new statement—interpretive or betraying—on the scale of a whole work. The other poems begin with so much more than Shakespeare alone and work everything to such a distinctly Eliotic purpose. Prufrock declares, "I am not Prince Hamlet." We may wonder if Eliot means to set this modern character against the romantic Shakespeare protagonist (what Prufrock himself seems to have in mind with his words), or if he means to offer, ironically, this modern mind as an account of the essential Hamlet—after all, Hamlet himself says, in a way, "I am not Prince Hamlet."[76] But there is something of the attitude of nineteenth-century French poetry in "Prufrock," something of the characters of Henry James and other novelists in the speaker; and the poem is so much "Prufrock," something entirely new. Shakespeare may be used in *The Waste Land* to evoke a past of beauty and passion, or a possibility of beauty and passion (and "Burbank with a Baedeker" is a striking small example of this, full of Shakespearean lines). But this is only to put Shakespeare in a category with other Elizabethan dramatists, Spenser, romance material, Indian religious writings, and more. The primary interest of *The Waste Land* is not Shakespeare (or Spenser or Indian religious teaching), but the whole set of contrasts and statements *as* a whole, the poem itself as a new thing.

Certainly Eliot's poetry from 1910 onward shows that he read Shakespeare with interest and seized passionately on details that he would use, with so much else, for his own purposes. I do not say that a criticism of Shakespeare is not to be gleaned from Eliot's poetry. But the task would require considerable care and room, with a focus on the center and unity of each poem on its own, and an address to the relation of thought and poetry much more daring than the caution Eliot so often repeats. In the final consideration Eliot's poetry, except for "Marina" and *Coriolan,* is not primarily Shakespearean. (One may say Eliot's criticism is not primarily Shakespearean—but on many occasions it *is* so, and what to do with a fragment of discursive writing, a comment here or there, is so much clearer than what to do with a fragment of a poem—a "transformed" allusion—other than see it in relation to the whole poem.)

4

The 1937 Shakespeare Lectures

These two lectures, "Shakespeare as Poet and Dramatist," were delivered by Eliot at Edinburgh University in 1937 and again at Bristol University in 1941. The talks subsume a good deal Eliot has had to say about Shakespeare, presenting a considered view that is Eliot's last extended discussion. He continues to refer to Shakespeare in the later criticism, stressing points he has made, for example, about Shakespeare's development;[1] about the use of poetry in the plays;[2] and about the functioning of the play as a whole.[3] More and more Eliot speaks about Shakespeare's "wisdom."[4] But the 1937 Shakespeare Lectures are the basis for these future references. Even though Eliot did not publish them, they are an appraisal he could stay with, not needing to pursue further issues.[5]

Eliot's purpose in the lectures is to describe Shakespeare's development as a matter of increasing concentration on the "what" that he has to say—the final meaning, the vision. Shakespeare allowed himself to focus more and more on the matter of "the poet's world," as it is called in the *Wheel of Fire* introduction; he seems in time to have drawn out of himself what he most wanted to say. Eliot speaks in the lectures of the "ultra-dramatic" and "musical" dimensions of the plays, which become more important in contrast to the elements of greatest theatrical appeal, what makes the most popular plays the most popular. But Eliot insists that what Shakespeare finally comes to—indeed, what he does at every stage—is entirely *dramatic*. Shakespeare does not escape the dramatic for the purely poetic or philosophical; instead, he reworks the dramatic itself. He makes it reveal the "ultra-dramatic" that is within it. The late plays leave behind one kind of dramatic appeal, but they exist to teach us what drama—and it is nothing but drama—can do.

The first, more general lecture addresses the issues of popular appeal and the musical or "ultra-dramatic," giving an overall picture of Shakespeare's career. Eliot begins a survey of selected plays with remarks on *King John*. The second lecture continues the discussion of individual plays with *Romeo and Juliet, Hamlet, Antony and Cleopatra,* and *Pericles,* allowing Eliot to thoroughly cover the nature of Shakespeare's art and the course it followed.

Eliot begins by saying that an extended look at Shakespeare has been "always something [he] wanted to do." He has been inhibited by feeling that he ought to read a great deal more of other critics; and he is still not satisfied with himself on this point. But he will speak. He *will* affirm that he has become more familiar with the plays, reading them and trying to see them whenever they are produced (Lecture I, p. 1). In remarks of later years, too, Eliot stresses that it is important to take opportunities to see productions.[6]

Eliot's point of departure is Granville-Barker's recent Romanes Lecture, *On Poetry in Drama,* a brief survey of English poetic drama up through the twentieth-century revival by Yeats, Eliot, Auden, and others that includes speculation on the proper use of poetry in drama. Granville-Barker insists that the poet must know his theater and that the poetry of plays must work in conjunction with action, the background the audience will see, and believable, intriguing characters as incarnated in specific actors. The most important aspect of drama is character—the conveying to us what specific characters are—and poetry above all other means is able, if properly used, to give us the "inner spirit" of characters.[7] Further, Granville-Barker suggests that poets are born, but that dramatists are made, by learning to use native poetic suggestiveness in the craft of playwrighting (pp. 39–40).

Eliot takes up Granville-Barker, insisting that poets also are made and that Shakespeare, in particular, developed as poet and as dramatist simultaneously. "Shakespeare was made a great poet by writing for the theater." His "verse improved, not merely in becoming more and more adapted to the purposes of the acted play, but absolutely" (Lecture I, pp. 1–2). For Shakespeare to become himself as a poet was to progress as a poetic dramatist. His is poetry which *is* poetic drama. Eliot notes that the period when Shakespeare began working was one in which blank verse was developing to take advantage of the subtle effects of speech, allowing "personages" to become "persons"—in short, a period in which the theater was becoming more realistic and appealing (pp. 2–3). Still, Shakespeare had "intentions of his own, intentions dramatic but not making for dramatic success." *Troilus, Measure for Measure, Timon* have a small public when produced, but offer as good dramatic verse as any of the plays—so do *The Winter's Tale* and *Pericles* (p. 3).

Eliot shows the complicatedness of the question of what Shakespearean drama is and indicates the sorts of qualifications that must always be made to anything one says about these matters. The term "drama" covers many things, and we get more of one thing in some work, more of another in other work; there is no need to fix on an ideal to the extent Granville-Barker does (pp. 3–4). There *are* Shakespeare plays that contain less interesting, less developed dramatic verse than others, but it would be hard to declare these plays less great than any others (p. 4; Eliot does not say which he has in mind). There are reasons for a temporary large appeal with some plays, but any enduring appeal is likely to indicate real dramatic virtue—five critics trying to prove *Hamlet* a bad play are not likely to persuade the world (pp. 4–5). Eliot names the most popular plays of his time as *Hamlet, Romeo, Macbeth, Othello, Julius Caesar,*

Richard III, Richard II, Henry V (probably a typing error for *Henry IV*, which is discussed in this regard immediately below in the lecture), *Twelfth Night, Midsummer Night's Dream, Merchant of Venice, Much Ado,* and *As You Like It.* There are reasons for popularity here that are insufficient for full appreciation of the plays: *Much Ado* is taken practically as a prose play; *Midsummer Night's Dream* is popular for Bottom, *Henry IV* for Falstaff—the pattern of different planes (as discussed in *The Use of Poetry*) is here only for the few (pp. 6–7). But the wit of *Much Ado,* and Bottom and Falstaff, are terribly important.

The convergence and divergence of popular appeal and the poet's—the poet-*dramatist's*—most personal "intentions" in the work of Shakespeare is a thorny subject. Before Eliot pursues a step-by-step consideration of Shakespeare's career, he says something in general about what dramatic poetry can do in the way of realizing a poet's "intentions." Speaking of dramatic verse and the "dramatic" in the usual limited sense of the term, Eliot says of the verse: "It introduces other interests and values, which exceed the demands of the 'dramatic,' if we keep 'dramatic' to its meaning of what is effective on the stage for an audience" (p. 7). There is no necessary sharp distinction between verse and prose with this larger purpose in view. Prose can give the "extra-dramatic" or "ultra-dramatic" interest, what is called a bit later "this 'poetic' interest" (p. 8), if only the dramatist is "interested . . . in the beauty of words and in what we may call their incantatory value; interested in language beyond the limited needs of expressing the thoughts and shades of feeling of a particular character at a particular moment" (p. 7).

But the realm to which verse or poetic prose takes us is not one of pure poetry or beauty, but a realm of "meaning" in the sense Eliot has developed in his criticism of the last ten years. Granville-Barker is wrong to say the poet's means are best used to persuade us characters are living creatures like ourselves with "inner spirit" (p. 8). Poetry does more. Or rather, "it all depends on the plane of reality on which we choose to take 'ourselves' as existing, whether that of social comedy or disaster, or that which we individually and unaided never reach" (p. 8). There needs to be "contact" between the characters of a play and ourselves, at the "starting point" of the characters' emotions. The "situations" from which their emotions arise must be "comprehensible to us in terms of our daily living"—it is difficult to become involved with the strange creatures of *Prometheus Unbound.* But the characters must exist "in a world to which we only penetrate when carried in to it by their words" (p. 9).

In Shakespeare and his contemporaries there are frequent speeches "in which a person is speaking, not out of character, but beyond character." No other character could have uttered the speech than the one who does, and yet the speech "has the impersonality of something which simply utters itself, which exists in its own life." We are reminded of Eliot's remark on "She looks like sleep . . ." in *Antony,* that it has an impersonal, "explicatory" force like so many utterances in Dante—though it is appropriate the character Octavius realizes what he does realize and speaks these lines as Octavius. In the first lecture Eliot mentions Vindice's silkworm speech, speeches of Chapman, Macbeth's words on the death of his wife, and the Duke's "Be absolute for death . . ." in *Measure for Measure.* The effect is that "we are lifted to another plane of reality, and a hidden and mysterious pattern of reality appears as from a palimpsest" (pp. 9–10). What we are engaged with goes beyond the "completion or perfection" of "the dramatic" in the usual sense. And for this larger purpose a plot or group of characters may be suitable though lacking ordinary appeal—here Eliot hints at those relatively unpopular plays of Shakespeare he has mentioned. We do not have to have tragedy with a murder or detective interest—what Eliot has frequently expressed thorough appreciation for, and an appreciation of it as entirely "serious"—nor do we need comedy with an imbroglio to be cleared up, nor even sympathetic characters (p. 10).

In sum, says Eliot, we have with Shakespeare—in plays popular or not, it is implied—two patterns "not divided": the "dramatic" and the "musical." "Dramatic" is used here in the limited sense already explained, and "musical" is virtually a synonym for "extra-dramatic" or "ultra-dramatic"—the terms are placed in apposition. "Musical" only goes beyond these other terms in suggesting, as in the analogy in earlier essays, the sensuous, total, and more-than-rational involvement of the audience in the "meaning" that is being posited. The "musical pattern" is beyond plot, character, and conflict of character—"a pattern of action in which characters do more than act of themselves, and of speech expressing more than what the characters know or know they feel" (p. 10). Eliot locates in the rhythms and imagery of a play, "in their recurrences and permutations," "a pattern of emotion beyond that which we ordinarily know as human" (p. 11). Here Eliot mentions Wilson Knight, who knew where to look and what to look for in the Shakespeare play, though he is sometimes over-elaborate and sometimes "endeavors to catch a falling star" (pp. 11–12). Thus, overall the poetry of Shakespeare, even if it is prose, takes us to a realm of meaning that is personal and individual, the pure Shakespeare, and at the same time impersonal, "beyond the human"—the intimation, we may say, of the permanent, of the perspective on life that is beyond life as usually understood. Shakespeare may work without the ordinary appeal of tragedy, comedy, or sympathetic characters. But so may he work *with* this appeal. And even the less commonly appealing plays are as thoroughly "dramatic" in the larger sense of the term—What are they if not that?

Eliot now turns to a stage-by-stage assessment of the development of Shakespeare's career. He says he would like to offer a simplified view of his career, not taking account of accident in the choice of subject for plays or in other choices about their writing. This view would involve first a period of gradual, irregular development while Shakespeare learned the possibilities of the stage and of language; then, in *Hamlet,* a fully developed dramatic skill—

in the limited sense—with the maximum of the "ultra-dramatic" that can be combined with what an audience likes best; followed by an increasing exploration of the possibilities of the "ultra-dramatic," neglecting the dramatic in the narrow sense (pp. 12–13). Having said this much, Eliot affirms that persistent study of Shakespeare's work makes the element of accident in its course seem negligible (pp. 13–14).

Using *King John* as an early example, Eliot speaks briefly about the development of blank verse and the state of the language when Shakespeare began to work. The account is much like that of the broadcast talks of 1929–31 on Elizabethan and Jacobean literature and Dryden. The dramatic verse of any period tends to develop toward an approximation to conversation; second-rate artificiality is what has to be broken through, the obsolescence of the previous period (p. 14). The individual poet tends to develop toward the contemporary idiom (Yeats is given as a modern example), "arriving at a more and more accurate setting down of the shades of feeling in a contemporary mind." (We are reminded of the discussion in earlier 1930s essays of how the poet comes to "write his time.") Overpowering emotions are permanently the same, but the poet cannot deal with emotion in the abstract. He gets the permanent in "particular instances in particular concrete and infinitely complex situations," which naturally demands comprehension of the conversational (p. 15).

Shakespeare began with a language that had recently become highly literary, "a huge and formless mass of words"; no one but Shakespeare could have coped with it. Eliot ventures an interesting speculation: What would English be if Shakespeare had not done his work with the language (pp. 15–16)? There is a natural speech of the peasant in his environment and a natural speech of the educated. The besetting problem with language is the speech of the half-educated, which is imprecise, "oratory." "The speech of the Elizabethan stage began as oratory; and Shakespeare transmuted it into language" (p. 16). Marlowe is said to have had magniloquence, with sometimes the "ring of speech"; but there is a lack of range. Shakespeare is superior in "smaller things"—setting down all the "shades of feeling." Shakespeare's mastery of the "smaller things" will "give his great tragedies, when he [comes] to them, a depth of meaning Marlowe would never have sounded" (pp. 16–17).

Eliot cites as a first striking example of what was new in Shakespeare, particularly in distinction from Marlowe, the figure of the Bastard in *King John*. Several lines are quoted of his speech in the first scene, upon his advancement: "Well, now can I make any Joan a lady, / 'Good den, Sir Richard!'—'God-a-mercy, fellow.'" Eliot remarks on the "humanity" of these lines, beside which the magniloquence of Marlowe seems shallow. The Bastard's way of speech is said to foreshadow Iago, Timon, Lear, Antony (p. 18)—the "human" and "small," "shades of feeling," are set down as a medium for the larger emotions and significance to take form in.

Eliot echoes the view of his old teacher, G. P. Baker, in proposing that full development beyond Marlowe was not possible in the chronicle play.[8] Eliot notes only the promise of "richness" in *Richard II*, as in the *Love's Labor's Lost* line "To move wild laughter in the throat of death," a sense of power as yet held in reserve. The chief larger interest of the early history plays is the general criticism of the whole "raving and cursing crew" of the Wars of the Roses—criticism implicit in the way the characters speak: in the style of the opening of *Richard III* (a mistake for *Richard II?*), or the balanced conceited style of *John,* or the Marlovian style (Lecture I, pp. 18–19). In sum, in Shakespeare's early work dramatic skill—in the limited sense—is not brought to its highest point, and of "*hidden music,* the under and overtones" there are only hints. The two qualities are not the same, though they have a way to go still where they develop together (p. 20).

The second lecture continues the survey of Shakespeare's career, beginning with comments on *Romeo and Juliet,* both its conversational and "ultra-dramatic" aspects. The versification comes to life with the appearance of the Nurse. It is Shakespeare's greatest contribution so far, after the early speeches of the Bastard in *John.* Old Capulet has it, the "gift of conversational verse"; Eliot quotes his speech in scene 5, beginning, "More light, ye knaves! and turn the tables up, / And quench the fire, the room has grown too hot" (Lecture II, p. 1). Eliot repeats his point that mastery of this mode was necessary for Shakespeare's greatest plays and highest dramatic moments to come. He notes that Shakespeare excelled all poetic dramatists in this mode, not just English ones. He makes the interesting comment that Shakespeare, with this achievement, "establishes the English language as potentially superior to all others for poetry" (pp. 1–2). The point, again, is close to that of the earlier broadcast talks; Eliot has more to say in this lecture (not detailed here) about the need of every writer to find the conversational mode for himself and about its presence in Blake, Burns, and later nineteenth-century French poetry.

Mercutio's Queen Mab speech, in the second passage, "True, I talk of dreams, / Which are the children of an idle brain," is said to anticipate *Hamlet* and *The Tempest* on dreams and imagination, or life as dream—however one wants to put it. With Mercutio on Queen Mab, Shakespeare imposes "as much strain as the action will bear, in order to convey something logically and dramatically irrelevant that goes beyond drama" (pp. 2–3). We are given an intimation not to be ignored, an unearthly perspective on the drama and its life in the conventional understanding. The Balcony scene is said to have "a musical pattern" from its beginning. Eliot notes the arrangement of voices soon after the lovers have recognized each other (II, ii, 70ff.), with Juliet's three single-line speeches against Romeo's three-, four-, and five-line speeches. Juliet's voice seems to "lead" like a musical voice, the whole pattern then finding release in a long speech of Juliet's. Eliot remarks "lightning" as a "keyword" in the scene, connected to the very swiftness of the play itself (p. 3). In the "musical pattern," we may say, the characters move according to forces behind or beyond the apparent—as conventionally understood—life of the drama.

Regarding *Hamlet* Eliot comments on the conversation and variety of the first scene, then deals with the popularity issue. He is led thence to some general discussion of where Shakespeare goes with the plays after *Hamlet,* plays more "objective," easier to take as wholes. The variety of versification in *Romeo* is not really "welded," but the first scene of *Hamlet* has variation of style with no sense of incongruity. The colloquial is developed beyond the monologue, as with characters of *King John* and *Romeo,* to quick dramatic dialogue. At the scene's opening "one looks through" the diction to see only the meaning, forgetting the distinction between poetry and prose, the poetic and the dramatic. Then there is the slower movement with Horatio and Marcellus, dignity and majesty with the appearance of the Ghost, the later "staccato," and, finally, the lyrical ending, "But, look, the morn in russet mantle clad," which serves a "musical" rather than a dramatic need (pp. 3–5). Thus, the conversational speech itself is worked into a musical pattern. We have the particular, concrete, complex situation, with its flow forward and its natural variety; and we have the hearkening to the dictation as from behind or beyond the apparent scene, which gives the lyrical outburst at the end as the proper conclusion to *this* series of rhythms, to *these* events. Horatio the character may want to feel as he does at the end, but Eliot suggests that he partakes of a larger, more general need than the idea of "his own" conveys.

As for the popularity of *Hamlet,* especially as opposed to later plays, Eliot says it cannot be due to a plausible story, or to the best constructed of plots, or to dramatic verse that is any better than what comes later. Rather, Shakespeare was able at just this point in his life, "to produce something that corresponds to a crisis in the ordinary man's life . . . Hamlet is a role in which every man can, in fantasy, cast himself." (It is the same process of audience involvement described in the early "Romantic Englishman" essay.) *Timon, Troilus, Measure for Measure, Antony, Coriolanus*—the "objective studies"—require of the audience a mature, sobered imagination; so do the last plays. "With the later characters you are not, so to speak, expected to identify yourself." With *Hamlet* Shakespeare gives us a statement of his problems more calculated to win interest—by the process of identification with the character—than the "resolution" that comes later. Here Shakespeare touches the imagination and feeling of the greatest number, after which he moves away "like a comet" into "his private mystery" (pp. 6–7).

Eliot goes on to explain that in the plays after *Hamlet* identification, in a sense, is asked from the audience, but identification with something other than ordinary life as ordinarily understood—what is still the case with *Hamlet,* he implies. The characters Lear and Coriolanus are not as "interesting" as Hamlet because we have to see them as part of a whole situation, not taking each scene "as it comes," but making an unusual effort to grasp the whole, which "requires as much familiarity and study as grasping a symphony as a whole" (pp. 8–9). The musical analogy is thus not only sensual but structural—or rather, as with a symphony, one works to be cognizant of structure almost against the tendency that carries one away in the senses. In the plays after *Hamlet* the principal emotion "tends to become something which exists only in the whole play." It is emotion "beyond the primary 'dramatic,'" "another plane of reality" than that. The *Romeo* Balcony scene expresses more than is in the awareness of the lovers; but it is not beyond character—it says what all lovers in that position would like to say. The first scene in *Hamlet* and the soliloquies do not require transcendence of the ordinary plane of living. "But the agony of Lear is something so intense that we can hardly divine it, or, as we do, we find ourselves becoming a state of feeling so overpowering that Lear himself disappears in it" (p. 9). We identify—if we come this far—not with a character but a "whole." Shakespeare makes us see through "ordinary classified emotions" into a world of emotion and feeling of which we are not ordinarily aware. "What he makes me feel is not so much that his characters are creatures like myself, but that I am a creature like his characters, taking part, like them, in no common action, of which I am for the most part quite unaware" (p. 11). The poet seems to lose interest in the ordinary planes of reality, to want to be "not *less* dramatic" but "*beyond* the dramatic"—or so Eliot feels after much "brooding" on *Lear, Measure for Measure, Timon, Troilus,* and the late plays (pp. 11–12). The interest appears in "a pattern of feeling of which the plot and characterization exhibit, so to speak, only the under side" (p. 12).

Antony and Cleopatra represents the complete achievement of conversational speech, the casting of a play, for whatever high things it has to achieve, wholly in this mode of the "concrete" and "particular"—the mode Shakespeare's contemporaries could use only in humble domestic situations and in flashes. The bringing of the general wholly into the language of the particular becomes, in a way, the very subject of the play—"a fusion of sordidness and magnificence is so essential a part of the pattern." The two lovers are "royal, magnificent, and without dignity." Antony would "reel the streets at noon, and stand the buffet / With knaves that smells of sweat." Cleopatra would "hop forty paces through the public street"; she was "commanded" "by such poor passion as the maid that milks." The sordidness and magnificence are not just contrasted but "*fused*" (Eliot's emphasis), the fusion being given by "touch after touch," with much suggestion in a word or two—as when Octavius responds to Antony's challenge to single combat near the end: "Let the old ruffian know . . ." (pp. 12–13).

Eliot quotes Antony's interchange with Enobarbus in act 1, scene 2:

> Fulvia is dead.
> —Sir?
> Fulvia is dead.
> —Fulvia?
> Dead.

The speech might be either prose or poetry. There is "compactness" "with behind it the beat of . . . hidden music" (the term is borrowed, I suspect, from Henry James's "The Figure in the Carpet"); there is connection to the human speech of the Bastard in *John*. "Only the poet who can say the common things, as common men would say them in daily speech, can say the greatest things." Shakespeare is likened to Chaucer in this respect; to the two of them "we owe our standards of English poetry" (p. 14). In the interchange with Enobarbus the "great thing" is said in the subject matter, we may say, the solemn news itself, and in the bringing to life of the hidden music—the demonstration that these men, speaking as men would in daily life, are *at the same time* entering into the ceremoniousness and echoing that belong to a rhythm beyond the daily as we usually see it. Here Eliot also notes that the "hidden" music becomes audible once in this play (the Soldiers' scene at night, IV, iii), as it sometimes does in the later plays, as if to remind us with a shock of what is really there all the time.

Now Eliot turns to the late plays, first with some general remarks on their purpose and procedures, then with commentary on the recognition scene in *Pericles*. Beyond *Antony* and *Coriolanus* one must be concerned with the "what" Shakespeare is saying, the "ultra-dramatic" itself (pp. 14–15). That is, earlier we are made gradually aware of the perspective beyond the apparent; now we are asked to focus on this perspective itself. There are no sharp distinctions; the later plays are implicit in the earlier, and the earlier are explained by the later. It is, again, like the whole poem of Dante, where the "Paradiso" is needed to explain the "Inferno" (p. 16). The late plays do present a challenge: "it is for us to educate ourselves until we can produce them and appreciate their production." The writer has

> seen *through* the dramatic action of men into a spiritual action which transcends it. There was always present—certainly from the period of *Romeo*—the perception that emotions are not sharply definite "things," with hard outlines; that the specifically "human" even is an abstraction of actions from a kind of continuum of emotion where the distinctions of individuality melt . . . a whole world of feeling. [p. 16]

The "music" of the *Romeo* Balcony scene, or the intimation of the Queen Mab speech, becomes finally an insistence on the "continuum" or "world" or pattern itself, from which proceed the personages and particulars of life in the plays.

The late plays show certain characteristics of technique. At this stage, says Eliot, dramatic action in the ordinary sense is inadequate for Shakespeare, and he tends to simplify characters, making them vehicles for something they are unaware of. We regard them and realize "we know neither what we do nor what we feel." The recurrence of vision and dream has deep significance in these plays. Eliot quotes Posthumus's lines after the dream in prison and the reading from the book he finds (*Cymbeline*, V, iv):

> 'Tis still a dream, or else such stuff as madmen
> Tongue and brain not; either both or nothing;
> Or senseless speaking, or a speaking such
> As sense cannot untie.

The intimation of Mercutio's Queen Mab speech becomes the form of life, Eliot is saying, which we are presented directly in these late plays (Posthumus goes on here: "Be what it is, / The action of my life is like it"). The versification of the late plays develops new possibilities; there is, for example, the word-play of the early plays, but with subtle and profound meaning. Arviragus's words on the disguised Imogen are quoted (*Cymbeline*, IV, ii, 52ff.):

> Nobly he yokes
> A smiling with a sigh, as if the sigh
> Was that it was for not being such a smile.

Clearly, this is not just cleverness or gallantry, but an effort—impersonal, we may say, with regard to the character Arviragus—to describe the ineffable quality of Imogen, who belongs to a special race of a world apart. Wilson Knight is commended for pointing out the use of symbols in these plays, but "*appreciation*" (Eliot's emphasis) is said to be not "conscious," recognizing each thing as it comes; there is a cumulative effect as in listening-through to a great piece of music. Still, "musical pattern" is an inadequate phrase: all the senses are used to convey something beyond sense (if not Wilson Knight's intellectually graspable significance). Eliot himself testifies in the lecture to a fascination with the *smell* of seaweed throughout *Pericles* (pp. 17–18). We begin with Lear and Coriolanus to understand characters through the whole play, and we do so now more than ever. It is irrelevant to compare the late heroines with Juliet. They belong, instead, to a world from which some emotions have been purified away to make apparent others, we may say, that relate most pertinently to the whole (p. 18).

Eliot calls *Pericles* "a very great play" and proceeds to comment on the recognition scene (V, i). We are given the speech of creatures who are "more than human." Marina's approach to Pericles is quoted:

> I am a maid,
> My lord, that ne'er before invited eyes,
> But have been gazed on like a comet. She speaks,
> My lord, that, may be, hath endured a grief
> Might equal yours, if both were justly weighed.

Eliot comments that as the scene progresses the two voices "are perfectly harmonized." There is an identity of experience between the two in the lines, rather than any individuality; the characters are "more than human," we may say, in this very identity of experience and voices beyond the individual. Eliot quotes Pericles' eventual "Now blessing on thee! Rise; thou art my child. / Give me fresh garments. Mine own!" With this, Eliot says, and with the emphasis on fresh garments of "Give me my robes" a few lines later, the scene becomes ritual. "The poetic drama developed to its highest point turns back towards liturgy." Only the vision of Diana could (as it does) end the scene (p. 18). The "what" Shakespeare is saying thus becomes the simplified, "more than human" characters and their involvement in the peculiar whole actions of these late plays—"senseless speaking, or a speaking such as sense cannot untie." Our apprehension of the "what" comes finally to be our involvement as in liturgy—a cumulative involvement, like listening to a great piece of music, but using all the senses for the sake of something beyond sense, something, even if it is beyond sense, still not subject to the intellect.

In closing Eliot reasserts that the verse of the later plays and the less popular plays of Shakespeare's maturity "is no less great as *dramatic* verse than that of what are called the 'great' plays." He reminds us that he has used the term "dramatic" in contrast to "ultra-dramatic," but he means "dramatic" finally to comprehend both these notions. What we have in the late plays is drama—personages and an action and involvement of the audience that is more than "conscious"—drama that the earlier plays *tend toward* with their perfection of the conversational and the dramatic in a limited sense, touching the feeling and imagination of the greatest number, with their intimation of something beyond the apparent. In the late plays "Shakespeare succeeded in doing what he set himself to do." Perhaps they are not to be made popular, "but if we recognize that the failure is in ourselves we shall have gone a long way." What is "latent" in the earlier work comes to the "foreground." "Without his success in the 'dramatic' he could never have found the way to what lies beyond it." The early and middle plays contain a "senseless speaking" which wants to come forward. Shakespeare had to achieve the "drama" of the early and middle periods in order to have an intimation of the "senseless speaking," the "poet's world," that he could present directly in the late work. "It is the dramatist in Shakespeare that makes him a great poet" (p. 20).

At the beginning and at the end of the lectures Eliot insists that Shakespeare's late work, the direct presentation of the "ultra-dramatic," is yet entirely "dramatic," and that it proceeds inevitably out of the drama of the middle period with its mastery of the conversational and its immediate connection to the lives of the audience. Eliot is very convincing with *Antony* about the "fusion," the entire at-oneness, of the conversational, the "small," the recognizable and down to earth, with the magnificent, the general, and the movement according to a hidden music—what Wilson Knight frankly calls the transcendent in this play.[9] But it may be felt there is a gap between Eliot's treatment of *Antony* and that of the late plays (*Pericles* in particular). Does he really offer the critical discussion to enforce his point that the middle-period drama goes on into the last plays, in fact dictates and forms their peculiar abstraction?

I suggest that Eliot poses his point as a problem. Ought we not to think hard, Eliot is saying, about the last plays as the inevitable next stage in this progressing drama? Perhaps it is impossible to put the connection into words. But is there not a great mystery here to be thought about? Eliot's prodding tactic is like that of the early "Hamlet" essay: Is there not something there in *Coriolanus* and *Antony?* A standard for drama besides the one we are accustomed to employ with *Hamlet?* Perhaps when we come to the "liturgical" recognition scene of *Pericles,* we may bring into play a life's experience of the relations of parent and child, what is made "dramatically" specific in more conventional terms in *King Lear,* say. Perhaps with Arviragus on Imogen's smile we may bring into play such experiences with contemplated ideals as are spelled out more purely "dramatically" with Hamlet and his various ideals, or with Antony and Cleopatra as they contemplate each other. Eliot challenges us to look again at the late plays themselves.

Eliot has a good deal to say about the perspective on life that is as if from beyond life—in drama the "ultra-dramatic," what we apprehend like a hidden music, what we know by participation as if in ritual. It is possible to regard Eliot as overenthusiastic here, given to the supernatural (perhaps to the doctrine that this life is relatively nothing), enjoying a sort of trance that rejects life. I suggest that, again, as with the idea of the dramatic in the late work, Eliot is speaking of something complex for which there are no words; he is trying to put us on the way to thinking about something. The perspective as if from beyond life comes out of the individual play, its drama (which it may have a good deal of in the conventional sense, as with *Hamlet* or *Antony*) and its details. Eliot does not mean to turn us away from these things—we ought to trust the critic so far who shows himself so sensitive to the raciness and tensions of the middle-period work and testifies to a preoccupation with *smell* in *Pericles.* Eliot's point here is like that about the Shakespeare songs in the essay on Marianne Moore: there is a gaiety by virtue of form with a solemnity of content, or a solemnity by virtue of form with a gaiety of content, and the copresence of gaiety and solemnity amounts to a perspective as from beyond this life. We must be taken in to the individual song and its dramatic context—the extraordinary perspective *consists in* this particular involvement on our part. So it is in the Shakespeare Lectures—their purpose is to direct us not toward a trancelike state but back into the plays, which may be seen differently than as they have been.

Eliot is preoccupied in the lectures with Shakespeare's career from beginning to end and regarded as a whole; and he is interested in a perspective in the work, on life as if from beyond life, apprehended as if it were hidden music. These interests come close to those of Eliot's creative work of this period, "Burnt Norton" (1936), *The Family Reunion* (1939), and the subsequent *Quartets* of the war years. Harry in *The Family Reunion* testifies that he feels

> That apprehension deeper than all sense,
> Deeper than the sense of smell, but like a smell
> In that it is indescribable, a sweet and bitter smell
> From another world . . . a vapor dissolving
> All other worlds, and me into it. [*CPP,* p. 252; my ellipsis]

And the assembled family members declare,

> In an old house there is always listening, and more is heard than is spoken.
> And what is spoken remains in the room, waiting for the future to hear it.
> And whatever happens began in the past, and presses hard on the future . . .
> There is no avoiding these things . . .
> There are certain inflexible laws
> Unalterable, in the nature of music. [*CPP,* pp. 270–71; my ellipses]

The play brings together the possibility of the characters' intimation as from another world, their understanding of the interrelatedness, indeed identity, of what has occurred at separate places in time, and the sense of all this perception as being at one with "inflexible laws" "in the nature of music." The characters in this play, with their possibilities of perception of life, are put in the same position as the audience to Shakespeare, with its attention to his step-by-step career and to his deepest essentials that become explicit at the end and recast the appearance of what has gone before. *The Family Reunion* is about the direct perception of life. This underscores the point that perception of Shakespeare, of art, is a way to the perception of life—"Shakespeare is like life," and art amounts to a stage of the understanding.

In "Burnt Norton," section 1, the bird in the rose garden calls "in response to / The unheard music hidden in the shrubbery." It begins to give the intimation, in this first scene, which the thought of the whole poem, arguably of the whole series, goes on to realize completely. Again, it is a "hidden music" that seems to generate the struggle toward a true perception and to be the thing that perception returns to. In "Burnt Norton," section 2, the poet speaks of the eventual understanding of what has actually occurred as parts of time. He comes to a sense of

> a new world
> And the old made explicit, understood
> In the completion of its partial ecstasy,
> The resolution of its partial horror . . .
> To be conscious is not to be in time. . . . [*CPP,* p. 119; my ellipses]

It is just as the individual plays of Shakespeare are to be understood eventually in the "completion" that is the whole. Of course, there is the paradox that the wholeness of Shakespeare is to be known only as we go back and "live through" (in the words of the *Wheel of Fire* introduction) the individual plays, one after another; as here in "Burnt Norton" it is said, "Only through time time is conquered" (p. 120).

The concluding section of "The Dry Salvages," picking up the lightning image from "East Coker" (and perhaps from *Romeo and Juliet*?), speaks of the access of knowledge as if from beyond life,

> the unattended
> Moment, the moment in and out of time,
> The distraction fit, lost in a shaft of sunlight,
> The wild thyme unseen, or the winter lightning
> Or the waterfall, or music heard so deeply
> That it is not heard at all, but you are the music
> While the music lasts. [*CPP*, p. 136]

This intimation is directed to "the impossible union / Of spheres of existence" (p. 136). The perspective as if from beyond life is only gained through details—sunlight, wild thyme, lightning, the waterfall—like the "chaos" of Shakespeare's middle plays. The perspective when it comes is like music "deeply" heard, as is the understanding that eventually comes with Shakespeare. Details of life, like individual plays, are charged with an appearance unlike what they have had. Smell ("wild thyme unseen") has the nature of "distraction" by more than what is immediate, as it has for Harry in *The Family Reunion* or the reader of *Pericles*.

There are surely many currents in Eliot running from his early years to the late 1930s to form the meditation of the *Quartets*.[10] Eliot's study of Shakespeare, long going on and completed in the 1937 Shakespeare Lectures, contributed very importantly to this work. Eliot moved from a view of the chaotic lifelikeness of Shakespeare's plays to a view of their coherence. He wrote in the 1927 "Dialogue" that one would not want the plays different from what they are but that they are disconcertingly out of control. Shakespeare for Eliot at this point is like life; and the place of Shakespeare in the poetry before the 1930s is like that of the other elements of life—everything is individually vivid, each thing heavy with a suggestion of significance, one thing not cohering easily with another. If Eliot is asking in this poetry for the poise and unity that are realized only in *Four Quartets*, then his progress in thinking about Shakespeare, from a view of anarchy to one of coherence and meaningfulness, must be seen as crucial to the growth that finally allowed the *Quartets*. The place of the study of Shakespeare in this growth ought not to surprise us when we consider how often Eliot calls Shakespeare a great artist and how often his criticism makes the point that the transformed realm of art is where issues of life are dealt with.

Eliot's criticism needs to be read as a whole. His major ideas are not to be found neatly set out in this or that place, nor are his assessments of writers—

Shakespeare, Dante, Donne, Flaubert, and Eliot's own contemporaries. What Eliot had to say about anything important to him is something he refines, qualifies, adds to. In short, he repeats himself, but with a difference made, in essay after essay. To read Eliot through is to see how important Shakespeare was to him, how much there was continually for him to think about with Shakespeare. Eliot's famous general ideas about literature take on a new form when we look at his discussion of Shakespeare. Until we pay attention to his particular comments on passages of Shakespeare, we have not really got straight Eliot's point about reference in language. Until we face his account of Shakespeare as the most lifelike of artists, who brought his anarchic material to a unity, we do not see fully what Eliot means by the work of art as transmuted life and ideas.

To read Eliot on Shakespeare is to understand Eliot better. But there is more to it. To read these essays is to understand Shakespeare better. Eliot refers to Shakespeare so often, and from so many different angles of interest, that one is made to think about the plays over and over. Eliot is keeping Shakespeare alive for us. And we are in the end brought face to face with a great Shakespeare critic. Here is an interesting mind on the broadest scale, the equal of Coleridge and Johnson, offering a developed and highly individual view of Shakespeare. Now we have this view to sympathize with, to try out, to allow to affect us in our own assessment of Shakespeare.

Appendix

Criterion Writing by Others than Eliot on Shakespeare and Related Subjects

Part 1: Articles of Historical Scholarship and Reviews of Scholarly Books

1. W. J. Lawrence, "A New Shakespearean Test," II, 5 (Oct. 1923), pp. 44–94—the use of calls for musical instruments in dating of texts.

2. J. M. Robertson, "The Evolution of Blank Verse," II, 6 (Feb. 1924), pp. 171–87—lineation, metric, and style in the period of Shakespeare.

3. J. M. Robertson, "The Naturalistic Theory of Hamlet," III, 10 (Jan. 1925), pp. 172–92—something of a defense of his earlier book.

4. J. M. Robertson, rev. Dugdale Sykes, *Sidelights on Elizabethan Drama,* III, 11 (Spring 1925), pp. 456–59—authorship problems, style tests.

5. E. H. C. Oliphant, "Marlowe's Hand in 'Arden of Feversham,'" IV, 1 (Jan. 1926), pp. 76–93.

6. W. J. Lawrence, "The Mystery of the *Hamlet* First Quarto," V, 2 (May 1927), pp. 191–201—Q1, for a country tour, combines the Ur-Hamlet with borrowings from Shakespeare's stage version; Q2 is the original form of the Shakespeare play.

7. John Dover Wilson, rev. J. M. Robertson, *The Problem of the Shakespeare Sonnets,* VI, 2 (Aug. 1927), pp. 162–67—account of Robertson's "disintegration" of the text.

8. W. J. Lawrence, "Double Titles in Early English Drama," VIII, 30 (Sept. 1928), pp. 35–46—they were not cumulative with revivals and revisions, but had to do with publicity.

9. John Middleton Murry, rev. G. Connes, *The Shakespeare Mystery;* Clara Longworth de Cambrun, *Shakespeare: Actor-Poet;* J. Dover Wilson, various editions, VIII, 30, pp. 134–39—Stratfordian/anti-Stratfordian problems; source problems.

10. J. M. Robertson, "The Scansion of Shakespeare," VIII, 33 (July 1929), pp. 635–41—even early Shakespeare is not perfectly regular; "the true metre is the rhythmic time-value of the total line" (p. 640).

11. W. J. Lawrence, "The Pirates of 'Hamlet,'" VIII, 33, pp. 642–46—Hertford's Men perhaps the country company who played Q1 (see above, item 6).

12. J. M. Robertson, "Shakespearean Idolatry," IX, 35 (Jan. 1930), pp 246–67—disintegrationist quarrels, response to E. K. Chambers, Dover Wilson.

13. W. J. Lawrence, "The Elizabethan Private Playhouse," IX, 36 (Apr. 1930), pp. 420–29—boy companies.

14. Leslie Hotson, rev. F. S. Boas, *Marlowe and His Circle*, IX, 36, pp. 555–57—commends the careful scholarship.

15. J. Dover Wilson, "Idolatry and Scepticism," IX, 37 (July 1930), pp. 631–41—attack on Robertson; defends consideration of the theater in criticism.

16. W. J. Lawrence, "The Secret of the Bad Quartos," X, 40 (Apr. 1931), pp. 447–61—country companies, 1592–1603.

17. J. M. Robertson, rev. E. K. Chambers, *William Shakespeare: A Study of Facts and Problems*, X, 40, pp. 290–99—reply on disintegration.

18. J. Dover Wilson, rev. J. M. Robertson, *The Genuine in Shakespeare: A Conspectus*, X, 40, pp. 537–41—against disintegration; defends Pollard, Greg, McKerrow, Granville-Barker, Chambers.

19. W. J. Lawrence, "Massinger's Punctuation," XI, 43 (Jan. 1932), pp. 214–21—examines a manuscript to explore what printers may have done to a playwright's punctuation.

20. Bonamy Dobrée, rev. J. M. Robertson, *Literary Detection;* A. J. A. Waldock, *Hamlet*, XI, 43, pp. 324–28—agrees with disintegration of *Macbeth* (incidentally throwing out the Porter scene, which Eliot often commends); praises Waldock's focusing on what is *critically* important.

21. Frederick S. Boas, rev. Leslie Hotson, *Shakespeare versus Shallow*, XI, 43, pp. 347–51—personal satire in Shakespeare.

22. L. C. Knights, "Education and the Drama in the Age of Shakespeare," XI, 45 (July 1932), pp. 599–625—education of all but the lowest classes would have enabled them to discern the sort of "pattern" elaborated by Wilson Knight.

23. L. C. Knights, rev. M. C. Bradbrook, *Elizabethan Stage Conditions*, XII, 46 (Oct. 1932), pp. 115–18—high praise.

24. G. Wilson Knight, rev. J. Dover Wilson, *The Essential Shakespeare*, XII, 46, pp. 122–24—Wilson is too free about Shakespeare's life and personal references.

25. C. L. Thomson, rev. Augustus Ralli, *A History of Shakespearian Criticism*, XII, 46, pp. 137–39—high praise, insists on need for scholarship and textual study to correct errors in criticism even now.

26. L. C. Knights, "Seventeenth-Century Melancholy," XIII, 50 (Oct. 1933), pp. 97–112—new psychology and death consciousness; social and economic conditions under James.

27. Bonamy Dobrée, rev. E. E. Stoll, *Art and Artifice in Shakespeare;* Wilson Knight, *The Shakespearean Tempest; Elizabethan Prose*, sel. Michael Roberts; G. B. Harrison, *A Last Elizabethan Journal*, XIII, 51 (Jan. 1934), pp. 326–28—Stoll does not go deep enough in understanding of the plays; Knight is now going too far.

28. Theodore Spencer, "John Marston," XIII, 53 (July 1934), pp. 581–99—the bitter satiric spirit of the age; comparisons with middle Shakespeare.

29. W. J. Lawrence, "Speeding up Shakespeare," XIV, 54 (Oct. 1934), pp. 78–85—there probably *was* act and scene division in Shakespeare.

30. A. L. Rowse, rev. Mark Eccles, *Christopher Marlowe in London*, XIV, 55 (Jan. 1935), pp. 322–23—circumstances of his later life.

31. B. D. [presumably, Dobrée], rev. *Plays of John Marston,* ed. H. Harvey Wood, XIV, 55—likely influence on the Shakespeare of *Timon.*

32. L. C. Knights, rev. J. Dover Wilson, *The Manuscript of Shakespeare's "Hamlet" and the Problem of Its Transmission,* and Wilson's edition of *Hamlet,* XIV, 56 (Apr. 1935), pp. 506–11—the bibliographical method only rationalizes the *taste* of the editor, which is to clean up ambiguities.

33. L. C. K. [presumably, Knights], rev. George Saintsbury, *Shakespeare,* XIV, 56, pp. 533–34—prosody separated from meaning—useless.

34. L. C. K., rev. G. D. Willcock, *Shakespeare as a Critic of Language,* XIV, 56, p. 534—Shakespeare's references to and implicit criticism of language.

35. Elmer Edgar Stoll, "The Dramatic Texture of Shakespeare," XIV, 57 (July 1935), pp. 586–607—this article is much in the spirit of Stoll's *Art and Artifice;* the thinking here, as in that book, is based on his early scholarship, but it goes entirely in the direction of emphasizing the artificiality and otherworldliness of the plays, and the use of poetry to create a repetitive "musical" texture (p. 598)—a point close to Eliot's in the 1937 Lectures and subsequent essays. Stoll calls *Coriolanus* "Shakespeare's greatest comedy," for its amount of *analysis* (pp. 595–97).

36. E. M. W., rev. Alfonso Par, *Shakespeare en la literatura española,* XV, 59 (Jan. 1936), pp. 361–62—the neoclassic taste in Spain.

37. L. C. Knights, rev. J. Dover Wilson, *What Happens in "Hamlet,"* XV, 60 (Apr. 1936), pp. 529–32—the words are reduced to statement value, the play becomes a detective story.

38. Frank Chapman, rev. Una Ellis-Fermor, *The Jacobean Drama,* XV, 61 (July 1936), pp. 739–42—mood of unease in the period; the book does not go far enough with individual writers—conventional in its literary estimations.

39. L. C. Knights, rev. Theodore Spencer, *Death and Elizabethan Tragedy,* XV, 62 (Oct. 1936), pp. 157–62—the method of literary research is wrong; the book uses only the prose meaning of poetry to discover attitude.

40. L. C. K., rev. *Shakespeare Criticism, 1919–1935,* ed. Anne Bradby, XVI, 64 (Apr. 1937), pp. 576–77—Robertson, Stoll, and Schücking are called "realistic"; reviewer recommends M. C. Bradbrook, Empson, Middleton Murry, Wilson Knight.

41. E. Martin Browne, rev. Granville-Barker, *Prefaces to Shakespeare, Third Series: Hamlet,* XVI, 65 (July 1937), p. 739—praises the effort to grasp the effect intended for the original audience.

42. L. C. K., rev. *King John,* ed. J. Dover Wilson, XVI, 65, pp. 757–58—discussions of textual revision.

43. Edward Sackville-West, "The Significance of 'The Witch of Edmonton,'" XVII, 66 (Oct. 1937), pp. 23–32—an interesting play of general themes, without the attraction of a great personality as in some of Shakespeare.

44. L. C. Knights, rev. Levin L. Schücking, *The Meaning of "Hamlet,"* XVII, 67 (Jan. 1938), pp. 365–67—*Character Problems* did pioneer work, but now the appeal to conventions avoids study of the individual consciousness informing the given play—the *use* of conventions.

45. A. R., rev. R. Pascal, *Shakespeare in Germany, 1740–1815,* XVII, 67, p. 378—use of Shakespeare in the coming to identity of the German middle class.

46. Bernard Blackstone, rev. Leslie Hotson, *I, William Shakespeare;* Oliver Baker, *In Shakespeare's Warwickshire,* XVII, 68 (Apr. 1938), pp. 540–42—Hotson highly speculative about Shakespeare's life and acquaintance; Baker excellent on life in Stratford in Shakespeare's time.

47. L. C. Knights, rev. W. C. Curry, *Shakespeare's Philosophical Patterns,* XVII, 68, pp. 574–79—fails by inability to trust impressions and discuss poetry as poetry.

48. Una Ellis-Fermor, rev. Clara Longworth de Chambrun, *Shakespeare Rediscovered,* XVIII, 71 (Jan. 1939)—was Shakespeare a Roman Catholic?

Part 2: Critical or Interpretive Articles and Reviews of Critical Books

1. J. Middleton Murry, "Romanticism and the Tradition," II, 7 (Apr. 1924), pp. 272–95—Shakespeare searches for a philosophical wholeness not apprehensible rationally; the late plays go beyond art, beyond comedy and tragedy (pp. 290ff.).

2. Herbert Read, "Psycho-Analysis and the Critic," III, 10 (Jan. 1925), pp. 225–28—Robertson does not account for the "personal intensity of expression" throughout *Hamlet;* Ernest Jones is recommended.

3. Virginia Woolf, "On Being Ill," IV, 1 (Jan. 1926), pp. 32–45—"rashness" is needed to read Shakespeare, to sweep aside what is said about him and make direct contact; "the brain rings and resounds with *Lear* or *Macbeth*" (pp. 42ff.).

4. Orlo Williams, rev. Middleton Murry, *Keats and Shakespeare,* IV, 1, pp. 194–95—Shakespeare is loyal to intense experience, reaches a state of gnosis, all life is a harmony.

5. Middleton Murry, "The Romantic Fallacy" (on Tolstoy's *What Is Art?*), IV, 3 (June 1926), pp. 521–37—*Lear* is used to argue that art gives a "life-conception" which is yet not "thought" (pp. 527–31).

6. H. P. Collins, "The Criticism of Coleridge," V, 1 (Jan. 1927), pp. 45–56—on Shakespeare, Coleridge is sometimes too speculative but great on the concept of the universal and particular and on the general point that Shakespeare is a philosopher, with a comprehension of life (p. 55).

7. Middleton Murry, "Towards a Synthesis," V, 3 (June 1927), pp. 294–313—Shakespeare in *Hamlet* obeys concrete experience while aiming toward a synthesis, religious awe (pp. 310ff.).

8. Bonamy Dobrée, rev. Wyndham Lewis, *The Lion and the Fox,* V, 3, pp. 339–43—the book praised as the only advance of late in Shakespeare studies except for textual criticism; Shakespeare offers a critique of action as such.

9. Anonymous rev. *Masterpieces of Chikamatsu (The Japanese Shakespeare),* VI, 1 (July 1927), pp. 88–89—Chikamatsu is quoted approvingly that "art lives in the shadow frontiers between reality and unreality"; the reviewer goes on, "the worth of art lies between reality and unreality."

10. T. Sturge Moore, letter on Shakespeare's imagery, VI, 2 (Aug. 1927), pp. 158–61—beauty arises from a whole of intellectual and other qualities.

11. Sturge Moore, "Towards Simplicity," VI, 5 (Nov. 1927), pp. 409–17—on issues raised by Wyndham Lewis and Middleton Murry; stresses the need to consider dramatic speeches in context of the action (pp. 413ff.).

12. F. McEachran, "The Tragic Element in Dante's *Commedia*," VIII, 31 (Dec. 1928), pp. 220–37—discourses on the study of free will and suffering of the individual in Shakespeare, Racine, Schiller; where the Greeks (or Ibsen) emphasize forces beyond the individual, and Dante concentrates on the *state* of collapse, separation from God (pp. 220–24).

13. F. McEachran, "Tragedy and History," IX, 37 (July 1930), pp. 661–70—tragic drama is philosophical, "valuing" what happens.

14. William Empson, rev. Elizabeth Holmes, *Studies in Elizabethan Imagery* (focuses on Shakespeare), IX, 37, pp. 769–74—the importance of every word in Shakespeare cannot be shown scientifically (as this book attempts to do), but only by old-fashioned appreciative criticism, which attempts to produce a like effect to what it talks about.

15. Bonamy Dobrée, rev. G. Wilson Knight, *The Wheel of Fire*, X, 39 (Jan. 1931), pp. 342–47—a very interested and sympathetic review.

16. Wilson Knight, rev. Ranji, *Towards the Stars: Being an Appreciation of The Phoenix and the Turtle*, X, 40 (Apr. 1931), pp. 571–74—Shakespeare's intuition of death's excellence, as in *Antony*, poems of Donne, Keats.

17. "H. R." (Read?), rev. *Coleridge's Shakespeare Criticism*, ed. Raysor, X, 41 (July 1931), pp. 786–87—it is the best Shakespeare criticism ever written, but it focuses too much on character and on the plays as a reading experience.

18. Middleton Murry, rev. Quiller-Couch, *Shakespeare's Workmanship*, XI, 42 (Oct. 1931), pp. 120–26—praise for the book, "nature responds to nature"; discussion of *Hamlet* as inevitable in its working-out.

19. L. C. Knights, rev. Wilson Knight, *The Imperial Theme*, XI, 44 (Apr. 1932), pp. 540–43—praises the concentration on the verse; states that the symbolic reading is, in fact, plausible for the Elizabethan audience (see Knights's "Education and the Drama in the Age of Shakespeare," described in part 1, item 22).

20. L. C. K. [surely, Knights], rev. Ellen Terry, *Four Lectures on Shakespeare*, XI, 46 (Oct. 1932), p. 166—the book is insignificant sentimental talk about characters, getting a great reception in the press.

21. L. C. K., rev. R. G. Shahani, *Shakespeare through Eastern Eyes*, XII, 47 (Jan. 1933), pp. 324–25—need to focus on the poetry, would answer Indian dissatisfaction with Shakespeare's religion.

22. L. C. K., rev. Logan Pearsall Smith, *On Reading Shakespeare*, XII, 49 (July 1933), pp. 710–11—the book needs more interest in language as the way to meaning.

23. A. Desmond Hawkins, "The Poet in the Theater," XIV, 54 (Oct. 1934), pp. 29–39—Shakespeare's characters are specific to his vision; still they embody universal experience, unlike Shaw's, where there is a focus on a single social situation (p. 32).

24. Wilson Knight, "A Note on 'Henry VIII,'" XV, 59 (Jan. 1936), pp. 228–36—praise for the play, which is seen to bring the transcendental intuitions of the romances back into the world.

25. A. A. W. Ramsay, "Psychology and Literary Criticism," XV, 61 (July 1936), pp. 627–43—praises Ernest Jones on *Hamlet,* proposes a view of *Othello* as self-doubting to account for the quick action of the play (p. 628).

26. Middleton Murry, rev. *New Temple Shakespeare,* commentary by M. R. Ridley, XVI, 62 (Oct. 1936), pp. 125–28—the critic does not see the characters in an imaginative context; Murry recommends A. C. Bradley for involvement in an imaginative experience.

27. E. Martin Browne, rev. Wilson Knight, *Principles of Shakespeare Production,* XVI, 62, pp. 143–46—Browne recommends Granville-Barker on the importance of the original style of production (see Browne's review of the *Prefaces,* described in part 1, item 41), but Browne is interested in Knight's way of production based on a central *idea* of the play.

28. Margaret Bottrall, "George Chapman's Defense of Difficulty in Poetry," XVI, 65 (July 1937), pp. 638–54—his intellectual theory should not obscure for us that he is a visionary.

29. Montgomery Belgion, "The Measure of Kafka," XVIII, 70 (Oct. 1938), pp. 13–28—discussion of *Measure for Measure,* its air of unreality that should tell us it will have a happy ending—a comedy of deception and self-deception (pp. 18–28).

Part 3: Reviews of Productions of Elizabethan Plays

1. Benjamin Gilbert Brooks, "The Maddermarket Theater, Norwich," III, 11 (Spring 1925), pp. 415–19—on *Othello* and *Hamlet,* "unity of dramatic tone in the acting," poetry given "its full value of emotion and rhythm"; speed helps with *Othello.*

2. Zoë Hawley, "'Midsummer Night's Dream' at Drury Lane," III, 11, pp. 419–21—fairies need to be represented more in movement than in decor, but this production is generally "alive."

3. Violet Ray, "Hamlet," III, 12 (July 1925), pp. 570–71—Barrymore subordinates his beauty to the part; the part is made to "live and breathe."

4. Violet Ray, "The Theater," IV, 1 (Jan. 1926), pp. 165–68—on *The White Devil,* Renaissance Theater Company: production brings out a "beauty" that transcends the tragedy and blackness; the "phases of the design" of a play are what production brings out and makes us remember. *Dr. Faustus,* Phoenix Society: the poetry is exquisitely rendered, one wants it ladled out thus, not glossed over like prose.

5. Michael Sayer, "A Year in the Theater," XV, 61 (July 1936), pp. 648–62—praises Gielgud's *Romeo* for visual and theatrical effects (pp. 659–61).

Notes

Shakespeare references other than Eliot's own quotations are to *Macbeth,* ed. Sylvan Barnet, New York: New American Library, 1963; and *Antony and Cleopatra,* ed. Barbara Everett, New York: New American Library, 1963 (both texts in The Signet Classic Shakespeare, gen. ed. Sylvan Barnet).

Introduction

1. See William H. Quillian, *"Hamlet" and the New Poetic: James Joyce and T. S. Eliot* (Ann Arbor: UMI Research Press, 1983), chapter 3, "Mr. Eliot and the 'Disintegration' of *Hamlet,"* pp. 49–77, esp. pp. 63ff. Beatrice Ricks's *Bibliography* lists seventeen items in the controversy over *Hamlet* and "objective correlative," going into the 1940s, 1950s, and beyond with pieces by Francis Fergusson, Eric Heller, and others—see Ricks, *T. S. Eliot: A Bibliography of Secondary Works* (Metuchen, N.J.: Scarecrow Press, 1980), pp. 174–75.

2. See, for example, John J. Soldo, *The Tempering of T. S. Eliot* (Ann Arbor: UMI Research Press, 1983), pp. 24–25.

3. L. C. Knights, "How Many Children Had Lady Macbeth?" and "Shakespeare and the Shakespeareans," both in *Explorations* (London: Chatto and Windus, 1946) (the essays date from the early and mid-1930s); M. C. Bradbrook, preface and introduction to *Themes and Conventions of Elizabethan Tragedy* (Cambridge: Cambridge University Press, 1935); D. A. Traversi, author's note to *An Approach to Shakespeare* (London: Sands and Co., 1938); S. L. Bethell, acknowledgments and chapter 1 in *Shakespeare and the Popular Dramatic Tradition* (1944, repr. N.Y.: Octagon Books, 1977); Henri Fluchère, preface to *Shakespeare and the Elizabethans* (1953 English version, repr. N.Y.: Hill and Wang, 1969) (Eliot is brought up later in the book as well in connection with language and convention).

4. Helen Gardner, "Shakespeare in the Age of Eliot," *Times Literary Supplement,* 3243 (Apr. 23, 1964), pp. 335–36; C. B. Watson, "T. S. Eliot and the Interpretation of Shakespearean Tragedy in Our Time," *Etudes anglaises,* XVII, 4 (Oct.–Dec. 1964), pp. 502–21; G. K. Hunter, "T. S. Eliot and the Creation of a Symbolist Shakespeare," in *Twentieth-Century Literature in Retrospect,* ed. Reuben Brower (Cambridge, Mass.: Harvard University Press, 1971), pp. 191–204.

5. Ronald Bush, *T. S. Eliot: A Study in Character and Style* (N.Y. and Oxford: Oxford University Press, 1983). Bush connects the lectures to Eliot's general thinking in the 1930s about "musical sensitiveness" appropriate in the audience of drama; about the possibility of miracle issuing from tragedy; and about "doubleness" of realms of experience in a work.

6. Debriprasad Bhattacharya, in an article in 1966, discusses a few of Eliot's persistent concerns with Shakespeare—verse and imagery, poetry that is dramatic, the artist and philosophy—but almost no reference is made to specific essays—"T. S. Eliot on Shakespeare," *Quest*, 50 (July/Sept. 1966), pp. 45–54. Phillip L. Marcus, in a 1967 article, shows little interest in the work before 1930, considering it generally negative; he speaks of Eliot's later interest in Wilson Knight, pattern in the plays, and the late phase of Shakespeare—but he has not seen the 1937 Lectures—"T. S. Eliot and Shakespeare," *Criticism*, XI, 1 (Winter 1967), pp. 63–79. James Torrens, in two articles of 1971 and 1977, looks chiefly for the use of Shakespeare to Eliot the poet; he finds the criticism to express the sort of mixed feelings about Shakespeare—a being impressed, but a recoil and fear of grasping the whole—that come to light in the allusions in the poetry—"T. S. Eliot and Shakespeare: 'This Music Crept By,'" *Bucknell Review*, XIX, 1 (Spring 1971), pp. 44–96, and "Eliot's Poetry and the Incubus of Shakespeare," *Thought*, LII, 207 (Dec. 1977), pp. 407–21.

  The longer study is Sudhakar Marathe, "T. S. Eliot's Shakespeare Criticism; Discovery and Advance," Ph.D. Diss., University of Western Ontario, 1982. This work is based on a thorough review of the criticism, and there is an appendix listing all the references to Shakespeare in the essays. Marathe has not been allowed to quote from the unpublished 1937 Shakespeare Lectures and so gives only a brief account of them, concentrating instead on "Shakespeares Verskunst," the German translation (not by Eliot) of a 1950 talk in Germany based on the 1937 Lectures.

Chapter 1

1. "The Letters of J. B. Yeats," *Egoist*, IV, 6 (July 1917), p. 90.

2. "Observations," *Egoist*, V, 5 (May 1918), p. 69.

3. "Contemporanea," *Egoist*, V, 6 (June–July 1918), p. 84. "Mr. Murry's Shakespeare," *The Criterion*, XV, 61 (July 1936), pp. 709–10.

4. "Reflections on Contemporary Poetry" (IV), *Egoist*, VI, 3 (July 1919), p. 39.

5. "'The Duchess of Malfi' at the Lyric: and Poetic Drama," *Art and Letters*, III, 1 (Winter 1919/1920), pp. 36, 38.

6. "Kipling Redivivus," *Athenaeum*, 4645 (May 9, 1919), p. 297.

7. "Tradition and the Individual Talent" (1919). I quote from *Selected Essays*, 1950 edition (repr. N.Y.: Harcourt, Brace and World, Inc., 1964), pp. 8–9. *Selected Essays* will be abbreviated *SE* in references in the text hereafter.

8. "Prose and Verse," *Chapbook*, 22 (Apr. 1921), pp. 6–7.

9. See, for example, Knights, "How Many Children Had Lady Macbeth?" and "Shakespeare and the Shakespeareans"; Bradbrook; and Bethell. See also Kenneth Muir, "Changing Interpretations of Shakespeare," in *The Age of Shakespeare*, ed. Boris Ford (Harmondsworth, England: Penguin Books, 1955).

10. "The Noh and the Image," *Egoist*, IV, 7 (Aug. 1917), p. 103.

11. "Studies in Contemporary Criticism" (I), *Egoist*, V, 9 (Oct. 1918), p. 114.

12. "Swinburne and the Elizabethans," *Athenaeum*, 1919. I quote from the reprinting, "Swinburne as Critic," *The Sacred Wood* (1920, repr. London: Methuen and Co., Ltd., 1976), p. 23. *The Sacred Wood* will be abbreviated *SW* in references in the text hereafter.

13. "Christopher Marlowe," *Selected Essays*, pp. 105–6.

14. "'Rhetoric' and Poetic Drama," *Selected Essays*, pp. 26, 27–28.

15. "Kipling Redivivus," p. 298.

16. "Reflections on Contemporary Poetry" (IV), p. 39.

17. "William Blake," *Selected Essays*, pp. 275–77.

18. See Quillian, pp. 11–21.

19. The meaning of "objective correlative" was a central concern of F. O. Matthiessen in *The Achievement of T. S. Eliot* (Boston: Houghton Mifflin, 1935). Recent studies have focused on the Bradleyan or Thomist dispositions behind Eliot's formulation; see, respectively, Mowbray Allan, *T. S. Eliot's Impersonal Theory of Poetry* (Lewisburg, Penn.: Bucknell University Press, 1974), pp. 76–93; and Edward Lobb, *T. S. Eliot and the Romantic Critical Tradition* (London: Routledge, 1981), pp. 47ff.

20. *Selected Essays*, p. 121. In the table of contents the essay is called "Hamlet and His Problems," as in the *Athenaeum* and in *The Sacred Wood*. On the page of *Selected Essays* where the essay begins, it is called simply "Hamlet."

21. "London Letter" (VI), *Dial*, LXXIII, 1 (July 1922), p. 96.

22. See Soldo, pp. 128ff.; also Herbert Howarth, *Notes on Some Figures behind T. S. Eliot* (Boston: Houghton Mifflin, 1964), chapter 5, "A Year of Diligence," pp. 126–27, 139ff.

23. Eliot's syllabuses are reprinted in Ronald Schuchard, "T. S. Eliot as an Extension Lecturer, 1916–1919," two-part article, *Review of English Studies*, XXV, 98/99 (May 1974/Aug. 1974). The "Elizabethan Literature" syllabus is found in the Aug. issue (99), pp. 298–302.

24. George Pierce Baker, *The Development of Shakespeare as a Dramatist* (N.Y.: Macmillan, 1907).

25. On Elizabethan drama in general see Baker, chapter 1, pp. 13–14, 21–25, 32–33. The standards for Shakespeare are spelled out in the chapter critical of the chronicle plays, pp. 147–49, 157–58, 171–72, 178–81, and chapter 6, "The Art of Plotting Mastered," pp. 181–220.

26. "Ben Jonson," *Selected Essays*, pp. 128, 131–34, 137–38.

27. "Philip Massinger," *Selected Essays*, pp. 187–88, 195.

28. See the 1818 "Course of Lectures," Lecture VII, "Jonson, Beaumont and Fletcher, Massinger," in *Coleridge's Miscellaneous Criticism*, ed. Thomas Middleton Raysor (Cambridge, Mass.: Harvard University Press, 1936), pp. 42–43. The lectures were first published in *The Literary Remains of S. T. Coleridge*, ed. H. N. Coleridge, 1836.

29. "The Preacher as Artist," *Athenaeum*, 4674 (Nov. 28, 1919), p. 1252.

30. "Dante," *The Sacred Wood*, pp. 165ff.

31. "'The Duchess of Malfi' at the Lyric," pp. 36–39. "Four Elizabethan Dramatists," *Selected Essays*, pp. 94–96.

32. "Kipling Redivivus," p. 297.

33. "Beyle and Balzac," *Athenaeum*, 4648 (May 30, 1919), p. 392.

34. "John Dryden" (1921), *Selected Essays*, p. 264.

35. Review of A. J. Balfour, *Theism and Humanism*, in *International Journal of Ethics*, XXVI, 2 (Jan. 1916), pp. 284–89.

36. Review of Wilhelm Wundt, *Elements of Folk Psychology,* in *International Journal of Ethics,* XXVII, 2 (Jan. 1917), pp. 252–54.

37. Review of R. G. Collingwood, *Religion and Philosophy,* in *International Journal of Ethics,* XXVII, 4 (July 1917), p. 543.

38. "Style and Thought," review of Bertrand Russell, *Mysticism and Logic,* in *The Nation,* XXII, 25 (Mar. 23, 1918), pp. 768–69.

39. "Eeldrop and Appleplex, I," *The Little Review,* IV, 1 (May 1917), p. 8. This spirit pervades the whole piece and the second installment in the Sept. 1917 issue (IV, 5). On the representation of Eliot and Pound, see Peter Ackroyd, *T. S. Eliot: A Life* (N.Y.: Simon and Schuster, 1984), p. 81.

40. "The New Elizabethans and the Old," *Athenaeum,* 4640 (Apr. 4, 1919), pp. 134–36.

41. "London Letter" (V), *Dial,* LXXII, 5 (May 1922), pp. 510–13.

42. "In Memory of Henry James," *Egoist,* V, 1 (Jan. 1918), pp. 1–2.

43. "William James on Immortality," *The New Statesman,* IX, 231 (Sept. 8, 1917), p. 547.

44. "A Sceptical Patrician" (review of the *Education*), *Athenaeum,* 4647 (May 23, 1919), pp. 361–62.

45. "William Blake," pp. 275–77.

46. "London Letter" (VII), *Dial,* LXXIII, 3 (Sept. 1922), p. 330.

47. "Ulysses, Order, and Myth," *Dial,* LXXV, 5 (Nov. 1923), p. 482.

48. "John Donne" (review of the love poems), *Nation and Athenaeum,* XXXIII, 10 (June 9, 1923), pp. 331–32.

49. A. C. Bradley, *Shakespearean Tragedy* (London: Macmillan, 1904), Lectures III and IV. The view of Bradley as the consummation of nineteenth-century criticism and as a major force to be reckoned with is taken in standard accounts of Shakespeare criticism. See Augustus Ralli, *A History of Shakesperian Criticism,* vol. 2 (London: Oxford University Press, 1932), pp. 200ff.; F. E. Halliday, *Shakespeare and His Critics* (London: Gerald Duckworth and Co., 1949), p. 264; and Arthur M. Eastman, *A Short History of Shakespearean Criticism* (N.Y.: Random House, 1968), chapter 9, "Bradley," pp. 186–204.

50. Schuchard, p. 301.

51. "Swinburne as Critic," p. 24. "London Letter" (VI), pp. 95–96.

52. See Ralli, sections on Stoll, pp. 254–59, 308–10, 322–26, 348–53, 513–22; Halliday, p. 265; Eastman, chapter 10, "Bridges, Stoll, and Schücking," pp. 205–18.

53. See Robert Speaight, *William Poel and the Elizabethan Revival* (Cambridge, Mass.: Harvard University Press, 1954). The best account of Granville-Barker's intentions is his *Prefaces* (collected, Princeton: Princeton University Press, 1946–47). On the whole movement, see J. L. Styan, *The Shakespeare Revolution: Criticism and Performance in the Twentieth Century* (Cambridge: Cambridge University Press, 1977). Of special interest are chapter 5, "Barker at the Savoy," pp. 82–104; and chapter 7, "Stylized Shakespeare and Nigel Playfair" (on the twenties), pp. 122–38.

54. On *Volpone,* "London Letter" (II), *Dial,* LXX, 6 (June 1921), pp. 686–91. On *Lear,* "A Commentary," *The Criterion,* II, 7 (Apr. 1924), pp. 231–35.

55. Elmer Edgar Stoll, *Hamlet: An Historical and Comparative Study* (Minneapolis: University of Minnesota, 1919). See esp. pp. 7–9, 63–69.

56. J. M. Robertson, *The Problem of "Hamlet"* (1919, repr. N.Y.: Harcourt, Brace, and Howe, 1920). I quote from pp. 72–73 and 74–75.

57. It is notable that another of Eliot's Harvard teachers, Santayana, produced an essay on *Hamlet* in 1908, stressing the composition in stages and the disarray of the play. But Santayana is very taken with the "texture," "imagery," and "happy strokes," and the projection after all of an interesting, "modern," idealist-romantic temperament at odds with the world. George Santayana, "Hamlet," *Essays in Literary Criticism*, ed. Irving Singer (N.Y.: Scribner's, 1956); see esp. pp. 120ff., 130, 134–36.

58. The 1937 Shakespeare Lectures (see chapter 4, note 5 for full citation of these lectures). The discussion of scene 1 is repeated in "Poetry and Drama" (1951), in *On Poetry and Poets* (N.Y.: Farrar, Straus, and Cudahy, 1957), pp. 48–81.

59. Schuchard, p. 299.

60. A. C. Bradley, "Coriolanus" (1912), in *A Miscellany* (London: Macmillan and Co., Ltd., 1929), pp. 73–104. I quote from p. 75.

61. Baker, pp. 286–91.

62. "Isolated Superiority" (review of *Personae*), *Dial*, LXXXIV, 1 (Jan. 1928), p. 6.

63. "To Criticize the Critic" (1961), in the volume of that name (N.Y.: Farrar, Straus, and Giroux, 1965), pp. 19–20.

64. "Hamlet and His Problems," *Athenaeum*, 4665 (Sept. 26, 1919), p. 941.

Chapter 2

1. See "Reflections on Contemporary Poetry" (I), *Egoist*, IV, 8 (Sept. 1917), pp. 118–19; rev. W. B. Yeats, *Per amica silentia lunae*, *Egoist*, V, 6 (June/July 1918), p. 87; "A Romantic Aristocrat" (1919), on George Wyndham, has remarks on Drayton, *The Sacred Wood*, p. 30; "Prose and Verse," pp. 3–10, has remarks on Dryden, Milton, Tennyson; see also "Modern Tendencies in Poetry," *Shama'a*, I, 1 (Apr. 1920), pp. 9–18.

2. "Andrew Marvell," *Nation and Athenaeum*, XXXIII, 26 (Sept. 29, 1923), p. 809.

3. Ibid.

4. "Lectures on the Metaphysical Poetry of the Seventeenth Century, with Special Reference to Donne, Crashaw, and Cowley," Clark Lectures delivered at Cambridge University in 1926. I quote from the carbon copy typescript in the Houghton Library, Harvard University, catalogued MS Am 1691.14, item 45; Lecture IV, p. 6 (this is the typed page number—these begin with "1" for each lecture; in addition, someone has pencilled consecutive page numbers from beginning to end of the work).

5. Clark Lectures, Lecture VII, p. 15.

6. "The Devotional Poets of the Seventeenth Century: Donne, Herbert, Crashaw," *The Listener*, III, 63 (Mar. 26, 1930), p. 553.

7. Letter under heading, "Questions of Prose," *Times Literary Supplement*, 1391 (Sept. 27, 1928), p. 687.

8. "The Tudor Translators," *The Listener*, I, 22 (June 12, 1929), p. 834.

9. "The Tudor Translators," pp. 833–34.

10. "The Prose of the Preacher: The Sermons of Donne," *The Listener*, II, 25 (July 3, 1929), pp. 22–23.

11. "Thinking in Verse: A Survey of Early Seventeenth-Century Poetry," *The Listener*, III, 61 (Mar. 12, 1930), pp. 441–42.

12. "The Romantic Englishman, the Comic Spirit, and the Function of Criticism," *Tyro*, I ([Spring, 1921]); the entire article is contained on p. 4 (though the page number is not given). The larger heading, "Notes on Current Letters," also includes Eliot's "The Lesson of Baudelaire."

13. "Marie Lloyd" (1923), *Selected Essays*, pp. 406, 407.

14. "'The Duchess of Malfi' at the Lyric: and Poetic Drama," p. 36.

15. "The Poetic Drama," *Athenaeum*, 4698 (May 14, 1920), p. 635.

16. "The Possibility of a Poetic Drama" (*Dial*, Nov. 1920), *The Sacred Wood*, pp. 62–64.

17. "The Poetic Drama," p. 635.

18. "London Letter" (III), *Dial*, LXXI, 2 (Aug. 1921), p. 214.

19. "Modern Tendencies in Poetry," pp. 17–18.

20. "Modern Tendencies in Poetry," pp. 9–18, passim. See esp. pp. 16, 17.

21. "Dramatis Personae," *The Criterion*, I, 3 (Apr. 1923), pp. 305–6.

22. "The Beating of a Drum," *Nation and Athenaeum*, XXXIV, 1 (Oct. 6, 1923), p. 12.

23. "Marianne Moore," *Dial*, LXXV, 6 (Dec. 1923), p. 595.

24. Jane Ellen Harrison, *Themis* (Cambridge: Cambridge University Press, 1912), containing Gilbert Murray, "An Excursus on the Ritual Forms Preserved in Greek Tragedy"; Jane Ellen Harrison, *Ancient Art and Ritual* (1913, repr. Westport, Conn.: Greenwood Press, 1969); Francis Macdonald Cornford, *The Origin of Attic Comedy* (1914, repr. and ed. with a foreword and additional notes by Theodore H. Gaster, N.Y.: Doubleday, 1961).

25. Most notably in "A Prediction," *Vanity Fair*, XXI, 6 (Feb. 1924), p. 29 (published in French translation the previous year, *Nouvelle revue française*, XXI, 122). See also "London Letter" (IV), *Dial*, LXXI, 4 (Oct. 1921), p. 453, apropos of Stravinsky's *Sacre;* and "Ulysses, Order, and Myth," p. 483.

26. See Piers Gray, *T. S. Eliot's Intellectual and Poetic Development, 1910–1922* (Brighton, England: Harvester Press, and Atlantic Highlands, N.J.: Humanities Press, 1982), chapter 4, "The Interpretation of Primitive Ritual," pp. 108–42. Gray has read Eliot's seminar paper and reports he is critical of interpretation, specifically of Jane Harrison's *Themis*, insisting on the primacy of the act as pure incomprehensible act—it is the point he repeats in "The Beating of a Drum," and indeed again in his introduction to Charlotte Eliot's *Savonarola* (London: R. Cobden-Sanderson, 1926, p. viii), apropos of the question of historical drama as interpretation of history. (Piers Gray discusses in the chapter cited the relation of Eliot's work on interpretation of ritual to his study of F. H. Bradley.)

27. "London Letter" (II), p. 686.

28. All quotations from "A Commentary," p. 235.

29. "The Beating of a Drum," p. 11.

30. "The Beating of a Drum," pp. 11–12. Again, Cornford does not provide a theory which Eliot simply takes over. Cornford is interested in the two distinct forms as developed to emphasize different aspects of the original seasonal ritual; comedy is to emphasize character; tragedy, plot—see Cornford, pp. 165–91. Eliot is interested, rather, in a unified or mixed form, which is Shakespeare's medium, allowing him the particular effects of individual plays.

31. "A Popular Shakespeare," *Times Literary Supplement,* 1255 (Feb. 4, 1926), p. 76.

32. "John Donne," p. 332.

33. "The Oxford Jonson," *Dial,* LXXXV, 1 (July 1928), p. 66.

34. "The Prose of the Preacher," p. 22.

35. "Andrew Marvell" (1923), *Nation and Athenaeum,* p. 809.

36. Introduction to Eliot, *Savonarola,* p. ix.

37. Sir Herbert Read, "T. S. E.—a Memoir," in *T. S. Eliot; The Man and His Work,* ed. Allen Tate (N.Y.: Delacorte Press, 1966), p. 28; Frank Morley, "A Few Recollections of Eliot," in Tate, p. 107.

38. "London Letter" (IV), pp. 454–55.

39. "Dante" (1920), *The Sacred Wood,* p. 168.

40. "Ben Jonson," pp. 131–32, 135–36.

41. "Turgenev," *Egoist,* IV, 11 (Dec. 1917), p. 167; "In Memory" and "The Hawthorne Aspect," *The Little Review,* V, 4 (Aug. 1918), pp. 45–46, 50–51 ("In Memory of Henry James" was previously published in the *Egoist,* Jan. 1918); rev. *Summer,* by Edith Wharton, *Egoist,* V, 1 (Jan. 1918), p. 10; "Tarr," *Egoist,* V, 8 (Sept. 1918), p. 105; "Beyle and Balzac," pp. 392–93.

42. "Four Elizabethan Dramatists. I. A Preface," *The Criterion,* II, 6 (Feb. 1924), pp. 115–23. "Preface to an Unwritten Book" is the subtitle in later collections.

43. "'The Duchess of Malfi' at the Lyric," p. 36.

44. William Archer, *The Old Drama and the New* (London: Heinemann, 1923).

45. "Four Elizabethan Dramatists," *Selected Essays.* See the beginning and end of the essay, pp. 91–92, 98–99.

46. "Chaucer's 'Troilus,'" *Times Literary Supplement,* 1281 (Aug. 19, 1926), p. 547.

47. "An Emotional Unity," *Dial,* LXXXIV, 2 (Feb. 1928), pp. 111–12.

48. "Elizabeth and Essex," *Times Literary Supplement,* 1401 (Dec. 6, 1928), p. 959.

Chapter 3

1. "A Brief Introduction to the Method of Paul Valéry," in *Le Serpent par Paul Valéry,* with a translation into English by Mark Wardle (London: R. Cobden-Sanderson, 1924), pp. 12–14.

2. "A Commentary," pp. 627–28.

3. "A Study of Marlowe," *Times Literary Supplement,* 1309 (Mar. 3, 1927), p. 140.

4. See "Andrew Marvell," *Selected Essays,* pp. 253–55.

5. F. R. Leavis pays tribute to Eliot on *Othello* in "Diabolic Intellect and the Noble Hero," 1936, which, of course, became an influential and controversial piece; see *The Common Pursuit* (London: Chatto and Windus, 1952), p. 151. L. C. Knights in "Prince Hamlet," 1940, takes much the same attitude as Eliot initiated, of not regarding the heroic protagonist at his own valuation of himself. Knights pays tribute to the Leavis essay—*Explorations* (1946, repr. Penguin Books, 1964), pp. 81–82.

6. A. A. W. Ramsay, writing in *The Criterion* in 1936 (see appendix, part 2, item 25), suggests that Othello be seen as principally doubting himself in a general way, which would make suitable the speed of the action; events proceed from a ready state of mind for catastrophe.

    The Cartesian problem is brought home to Shakespeare's protagonists by Stanley Cavell in recent and forthcoming work. See *The Claim of Reason* (Oxford and N.Y.: Oxford University Press, 1979), which concludes with a discussion of *Othello,* pp. 481–96; also "*Coriolanus* and Interpretations of Politics," in *Themes out of School* (San Francisco: North Point Press, 1984), pp. 60–96. The Renaissance sceptical problematic is discussed with regard to Hamlet and to Leontes in *The Winter's Tale* in papers that have been given as public lectures, due to be published by Cambridge University Press.

7. Wyndham Lewis, *The Lion and the Fox* (1927, repr. London: Methuen, 1966). See esp. the introduction, pp. 13–17, and part 4, chapter 3, "Shakespeare's Work as 'A Criticism of Action,'" pp. 159–65.

8. "The Lion and the Fox," *Twentieth Century Verse,* 6/7 (Nov./Dec. 1937), pp. 6–9.

9. *The Lion and the Fox,* p. 190. The speech is discussed on pp. 190–93.

10. "Mr. Murry's Shakespeare," pp. 708–10.

11. "A Note on Poetry and Belief," *The Enemy,* I (Jan. 1927), pp. 15–17.

12. "Literature, Science, and Dogma," *Dial,* LXXXII, 3 (Mar. 1927), pp. 239–43.

13. Ibid.

14. *The Lion and the Fox,* introduction, p. 21.

15. As in Knights's "Prince Hamlet," and Leavis's "Diabolic Intellect."

16. "Dante," *Selected Essays,* pp. 199–237. For a crucial passage on "poetic creation," see p. 209, on the Ulysses episode as compared to portraits of Dante's contemporaries.

17. Preface to the 1928 edition, *The Sacred Wood,* p. x.

18. Preface to *For Lancelot Andrewes* (London: Faber and Gwyer, 1928), pp. ix–x.

19. Preface to *After Strange Gods* (N.Y.: Harcourt, Brace, 1934), pp. 9–12.

20. *After Strange Gods,* Lecture I, p. 24.

21. "The Frontiers of Criticism" (1956), in *On Poetry and Poets,* pp. 113–31; "To Criticize the Critic," in the volume of that name, pp. 11–26.

22. "Mr. Middleton Murry's Synthesis," *The Criterion,* VI, 4 (Oct. 1927), p. 344.

23. Introduction to Ezra Pound, *Selected Poems,* ed. with an introduction by T. S. Eliot (1928, new ed. 1948, repr. London: Faber and Faber, 1952), p. 20.

24. Introduction to Eliot, *Savonarola,* p. x.

25. G. Wilson Knight, *The Wheel of Fire* (1930, new edition 1949, repr. London: Methuen, 1960), pp. 4, 11. The book is abbreviated *WF* in references in the text hereafter.

26. G. Wilson Knight, "T. S. Eliot: Some Literary Impressions," in Tate, p. 245.

27. Ibid., p. 247.

28. Knight, *The Wheel of Fire*, p. 16; Eliot, introduction to *The Wheel of Fire*, p. xx. Eliot does not mention Colin Still in the criticism prior to this. But Still's study of *The Tempest* (1921) has been suggested as a major inspiration for *The Waste Land*—Ronald Tamplin, "*The Tempest* and *The Waste Land*," *American Literature*, XXXIX, 3 (Nov. 1967), pp. 352–72; see my discussion at the end of this chapter.

29. Knight, "T. S. Eliot: Some Literary Impressions," p. 246.

30. G. Wilson Knight, "Myth and Miracle" (1928), repr. in *The Crown of Life* (1947, repr. London: Methuen, 1966), pp. 9–31.

31. Knight, "Myth and Miracle," pp. 14–17, passim.

32. G. Wilson Knight, "King Lear and the Comedy of the Grotesque," *The Wheel of Fire*, pp. 160–76. "A shifting flash of comedy across the pain of the purely tragic both increases the tension and suggests, vaguely, a resolution and a purification. The comic and the tragic rest both on the idea of incompatibilities, and are also, themselves, mutually exclusive; therefore to mingle them is to add to the meaning of each for the result is then but a new sublime incongruity" (p. 160).

33. Knight, "T. S. Eliot: Some Literary Impressions," p. 246.

34. See esp. *The Wheel of Fire*, chapters 3 and 4, pp. 47–96.

35. Eliot recommends Knight in "John Ford" (1932), *Selected Essays*, p. 171; "Mr. Murry's Shakespeare," p. 710; "The Lion and the Fox," p. 6. The recommendation of Knight, with reservations, occurs twice in the Shakespeare Lectures: Lecture I, pp. 11–12, and Lecture II, p. 17 (see chapter 4, note 5 for full citation of these lectures).

36. Clark Lectures, Lecture V, pp. 10–16. On Chapman, see "Wanley and Chapman," *Times Literary Supplement*, 1250 (Dec. 31, 1925), p. 907. The same doubleness is spoken of in the 1935 "Marston" essay, where the effect in Marston is compared to Chapman and Dostoyevsky—"John Marston," *Elizabethan Dramatists* (London: Faber, 1963), pp. 161–62.

37. Knight, "T. S. Eliot: Some Literary Impressions," p. 247.

38. "Poetry and Propaganda," *Bookman*, LXX, 6 (Feb. 1930), p. 600.

39. "Poetry and Propaganda," pp. 601–2.

40. Stephen Spender, "Remembering Eliot," in Tate, p. 54.

41. Knight, *The Wheel of Fire*, chapter 2, "The Embassy of Death: An Essay on Hamlet," pp. 17–46.

42. "Dryden the Dramatist," in *John Dryden* (N.Y.: Terence and Elsa Holliday, 1932), pp. 32–34. This book consists of three talks by Eliot on Dryden, somewhat revised from the originals, which are published in *The Listener* of 1931.

43. "The Music of Poetry" (1942), *On Poetry and Poets*, pp. 17–33.

44. Eliot must be referring to "Myth and Miracle," where the recognitions are seen to admit the characters—and audience—to the experience of a general transcendent love. Perhaps Eliot had seen *The Shakespearian Tempest*, published in 1932, which has a chapter on the final plays outlining the contrasting storm and music imagery roughly on the lines of mortal life versus the transcendent and eternal (*The Shakespearian Tempest* [repr. London: Methuen, 1953], pp. 218–66).

45. Lecture V, "Shelley and Keats," *The Use of Poetry and the Use of Criticism* (1933, repr. London: Faber and Faber, 1964), pp. 98–102. This book is abbreviated *UPUC* in references in the text hereafter.

46. "Shakespearian Criticism I. From Dryden to Coleridge," in *A Companion to Shakespeare Studies*, ed. Harley Granville-Barker and G. B. Harrison (Cambridge: Cambridge University Press, 1934), pp. 297–99.

47. "The Three Voices of Poetry" (1953), *On Poetry and Poets*, pp. 96–112.

48. "Wilkie Collins and Dickens," *Selected Essays*, pp. 409–18. See esp. pp. 409–10, 417–18.

49. "Audiences, Producers, Plays, Poets," *New Verse*, 18 (Dec. 1935), pp. 3–4.

50. "The Need for Poetic Drama," *The Listener*, XVI, 411 (Nov. 25, 1936), pp. 994–95.
    Carol H. Smith in *T. S. Eliot's Dramatic Theory and Practice* (Princeton: Princeton University Press, 1963) traces through Eliot's own plays his interest in popular theater as a socially unifying force, his motive being to bring the highest reaches of "meaning" into the realm of everyone's interest in entertainment and melodrama. See, for example, the discussion of *Sweeney Agonistes* (pp. 53–56), which brings up *The Use of Poetry* passage on levels of understanding.
    Another main theme of Smith's book is Eliot's use in the plays of the Greek Ur-dramatic ritual pattern and prototypical personages as described by Cornford (the discussion of *Sweeney*, again, is typical, pp. 39–47, 61ff.). I have suggested that Eliot did not take over Cornford's account of the *details* of ritual for the comments in the twenties on the ritual-like in Shakespeare and the poetic drama in general. It would seem that Eliot's turn to the Greeks for his own work was part of a deliberate effort to get away from Shakespeare and the great achievement of the poetic drama in English, to attempt something fresh. In "The Need for Poetic Drama" Eliot speaks of the need to get away from Shakespeare, to use *Everyman* and the Greeks.

51. "Audiences, Producers, Plays, Poets," p. 4.

52. "The Need for Poetic Drama," p. 994.

53. Introduction to Djuna Barnes, *Nightwood* (1937, repr. N.Y.: New Directions, 1961), pp. xi–xvi. See esp. pp. xii, xv–xvi.

54. *John Dryden*, pp. 60–61.

55. "Shakespearian Criticism I. From Dryden to Coleridge," in Granville-Barker, *A Companion to Shakespeare Studies*, pp. 294–96.

56. *John Dryden*, p. 12.

57. Introduction to Marianne Moore, *Selected Poems* (N.Y.: Macmillan, 1935), pp. xiii–xiv.

58. *John Dryden*, pp. 29–32.

59. "Milton I," *On Poetry and Poets*, p. 158.

60. See, for example, the early discussion by F. R. Leavis in *New Bearings in English Poetry* (1932, repr. Ann Arbor: University of Michigan Press, 1964), pp. 129–32; and the recent discussion in Bush, pp. 166–69.

61. G. Wilson Knight, "T. S. Eliot: Some Literary Impressions," pp. 246–47.

62. Knight, "Myth and Miracle," pp. 14–19.

63. Elspeth Cameron, in "T. S. Eliot's 'Marina': An Exploration," *Queen's Quarterly*, LXXVII, 2 (Summer 1970), pp. 180–89, sees the poem as decidedly under the influence of Knight.

She stresses the theme of creating a work of art and notes that Knight speaks of Marina in the Shakespeare as being herself a work of art in his 1947 essay on the play in *The Crown of Life*.

64. Knight, "T. S. Eliot: Some Literary Impressions," pp. 247–48; "The Royal Occupation: An Essay on *Coriolanus*," *The Imperial Theme* (1931, repr. London: Methuen, 1965), pp. 154–98.

65. Lewis, *The Lion and the Fox,* pp. 235–46.

66. *The Complete Poems and Plays 1909–1950* (repr. 1962, N.Y.: Harcourt, Brace, and World), p. 86. The book is abbreviated *CPP* in further references in the text.

67. See, for example, Grover Smith, *T. S. Eliot's Poetry and Plays: A Study in Sources and Meaning* (1956, second ed. Chicago and London: University of Chicago Press, 1974); A. D. Moody, *Thomas Stearns Eliot: Poet* (Cambridge: Cambridge University Press, 1979).

68. Margaret Morton Blum, "The *Fool* in 'The Lovesong of J. Alfred Prufrock'" (refers to Yorick), *Modern Language Notes*, LXXII, 6 (June 1957), pp. 424–26; Robert F. Fleissner, "'Prufrock,' Pater, and *Richard II:* Retracing a Denial of Princeship," *American Literature*, XXXVIII, 1 (Mar. 1966), pp. 120–23; Fleissner, "Prufrock's Ricardian Posture," *Research Studies*, XLVII, 1 (Mar. 1979), pp. 27–36; Robert Seiler, "Prufrock and Hamlet," *English*, XXI, 110 (Summer 1972), pp. 41–43.

69. John A. Major, "Eliot's 'Gerontion' and *As You Like It*," *Modern Language Notes*, LXXIV, 1 (Jan. 1959), pp. 28–31.

70. Paul Fussell, Jr., "A Note on 'The Hollow Men,'" *Modern Language Notes*, LXV, 4 (Apr. 1950), pp. 254–55; Robert F. Gleckner, "Eliot's 'The Hollow Men' and Shakespeare's *Julius Caesar*," *Modern Language Notes*, LXXV, 1 (Jan. 1960), pp. 26–28; Sidney J. Krause, "Hollow Men and False Horses," *Texas Studies in Literature and Language*, II, 3 (Autumn 1960), pp. 368–77.

71. Harry M. Schwalb, "Eliot's 'A Game of Chess,'" *The Explicator*, XI, 6 (Apr. 1953), item 46; Bernard Harris, "'This music crept by me': Shakespeare and Wagner" (transforming power of art), in "*The Waste Land*' in Different Voices, ed. A. D. Moody (London: Edward Arnold, 1974), pp. 105–16; Gayle Green, "Shakespeare's *Tempest* and Eliot's *Waste Land*: 'What the Thunder Said'" (transforming power of art), *Orbis Litterarum*, XXXIV, 4 (1979), pp. 287–300; Denise T. Askin, "*The Waste Land*'s Missing Hanged Man: A Source in *The Tempest*" (the Boatswain; in *The Waste Land* death by water *is* to be feared, because there is no possibility of restoration), *English Language Notes*, XVIII, 2 (Dec. 1980), pp. 130–31; Peter Milward, "Shakespeare in *The Waste Land*" (*Tempest*, but also "dust" and empty conversations of *Hamlet*, despair and fear of *Macbeth*, music as in numerous plays), in *Poetry and Drama in the Age of Shakespeare*, ed. Milward and Tetsuo Anzai (Tokyo: Renaissance Institute, 1982), pp. 218–26.

72. Ronald Tamplin, "*The Tempest* and *The Waste Land*," *American Literature*, XXXIX, 3 (Nov. 1967), pp. 352–72.

73. James Torrens, S. J., "T. S. Eliot and Shakespeare: 'This Music Crept By,'" *Bucknell Review*, XIX, 1 (Spring 1971), pp. 77–96; "Eliot's Poetry and the Incubus of Shakespeare," *Thought*, LII, 207 (Dec. 1977), pp. 407–21.

74. Gary H. Wilson, "The Shakespearian Design of T. S. Eliot's Poetry," Ph.D. Diss., Temple University, 1973.

75. Grover Smith, p. 209; Moody, p. 180.

76.   See Quillian's discussion in chapters 1 and 3 of *"Hamlet" and the New Poetic*.

Chapter 4

1.   See "Yeats" (1940), *On Poetry and Poets,* pp. 297–98; "The Music of Poetry" (1942), p. 29.

2.   Introduction to Bethell, pp. ix–x; "The Aims of Poetic Drama," *Adam,* XVII, 200 (Nov. 1949), pp. 10–16, revised as "Poetry and Drama" (1951), *On Poetry and Poets,* pp. 75–95.

3.   "Yeats," p. 305; "'The Duchess of Malfy,'" *The Listener,* XXVI, 675 (Dec. 18, 1941), pp. 825–26; "The Three Voices of Poetry" (1953), p. 104.

4.   See "The Social Function of Poetry" (1945), *On Poetry and Poets,* pp. 3–16; "Poetry and Drama," the concluding pages; preface to Leone Vivante, *English Poetry* . . . (London: Faber and Faber, 1950), pp. vii–xi; "Goethe as the Sage" (1955), *On Poetry and Poets,* pp. 240–64; "The Frontiers of Criticism" (1956), p. 128.

5.   The Shakespeare Lectures exist in a typescript at Houghton Library, Harvard University; the cataloguing is b MS Am 1691, item 32. Page numbers begin again at "1" for the second lecture.
      Parts of the lectures on scenes from *Romeo* and *Hamlet* are used again in "The Aims of Poetic Drama" and "Poetry and Drama" (see note 2 above). Eliot delivered a shortened version of the lectures as one lecture in Germany in 1950, which was published there translated into German (not by Eliot)—"Shakespeares Verskunst," *Der Monat,* II, 20 (May 1950), pp. 198–207, no translator identified. Donald Gallup names the translator as Gerhard Hensel in *T. S. Eliot: A Bibliography* (London: Faber and Faber, 1969), p. 290, item D238.

6.   Introduction to Bethell, p. viii; Eliot quarrels with Granville-Barker in a respectful way in the lectures, but here he recommends the *Prefaces*. See also the foreword to Fluchère, pp. 5–6; here too is a compliment for Granville-Barker.

7.   Harley Granville-Barker, *On Poetry in Drama* (London: Sidgwick and Jackson, 1937). See esp. pp. 16–19, 28–39.

8.   Baker, chapter 4, "The Chronicle Plays," pp. 142–81; see esp. pp. 171–75, 178–81.

9.   G. Wilson Knight, "The Transcendental Humanism of *Antony and Cleopatra*" and "The Diadem of Love: An Essay on *Antony and Cleopatra*," *The Imperial Theme,* pp. 199–326.

10.   Two studies particularly good on qualities of Eliot's mind and art in the earlier years that seem to lead inevitably to the later formulations, are Northrop Frye, *T. S. Eliot* (N.Y.: Grove Press, 1963), and Lyndall Gordon, *Eliot's Early Years* (Oxford and N.Y.: Oxford University Press, 1977).

Bibliography

Works by Eliot

Collections and Other Books

After Strange Gods. New York: Harcourt, Brace, 1934.
The Complete Poems and Plays 1909–1950. N.Y.: Harcourt, Brace, and World, repr. 1962. Abbreviated *CPP* in references in the text.
Elizabethan Dramatists. London: Faber and Faber, 1963.
For Lancelot Andrewes. London: Faber and Gwyer, 1928.
John Dryden. N.Y.: Terence and Elsa Holliday, 1932.
On Poetry and Poets. N.Y.: Farrar, Straus, and Cudahy, 1957.
The Sacred Wood. 1920, repr. London: Methuen, 1976. Abbreviated *SW.*
Selected Essays. 1950 ed., repr. N.Y.: Harcourt, Brace, and World, 1964. Abbreviated *SE.*
To Criticize the Critic. N.Y.: Farrar, Straus, and Giroux, 1965.
The Use of Poetry and the Use of Criticism. 1933, repr. London: Faber and Faber, 1964. Abbreviated *UPUC.*

Unpublished Work

"Lectures on the Metaphysical Poetry of the Seventeenth Century, with Special Reference to Donne, Crashaw, and Cowley," the Clark Lectures delivered at Cambridge University in 1926. Houghton Library, Harvard University, MS Am 1691.14, item 45.
"Shakespeare as Poet and Dramatist" (two lectures) delivered at Edinburgh in 1937. Houghton Library, Harvard University, b MS Am 1691, item 32.

Contributions to Books

"A Brief Introduction to the Method of Paul Valéry," in *Le Serpent par Paul Valéry,* with an English translation by Mark Wardle. London: R. Cobden-Sanderson, 1924.
Introduction to Charlotte Eliot, *Savonarola.* London: R. Cobden-Sanderson, 1926.
Introduction to Ezra Pound, *Selected Poems,* ed. T. S. Eliot. 1928, new ed. 1948, repr. London: Faber and Faber, 1952.
Introduction to G. Wilson Knight, *The Wheel of Fire.* 1930, repr. London: Methuen, 1960.
"Shakespeare Criticism I. From Dryden to Coleridge," in *A Companion to Shakespeare Studies,* ed. Harley Granville-Barker and G. B. Harrison. Cambridge: Cambridge University Press, 1934.
Introduction to Marianne Moore, *Selected Poems.* N.Y.: Macmillan, 1935.
Introduction to Djuna Barnes, *Nightwood.* 1937, repr. N.Y.: New Directions, 1961.
Introduction to S. L. Bethell, *Shakespeare and the Popular Dramatic Tradition.* 1944, repr. N.Y.: Octagon Books, 1977.
Preface to Leone Vivante, *English Poetry.* London: Faber and Faber, 1950.
Foreword to Henri Fluchère, *Shakespeare and the Elizabethans.* 1953 English version, repr. N.Y.: Hill and Wang, 1969.

Contributions to Periodicals

1916

rev. A. J. Balfour, *Theism and Humanism. International Journal of Ethics*, XXVI, 2 (Jan. 1916), pp. 284–89.

1917

rev. Wilhelm Wundt, *Elements of Folk Psychology. International Journal of Ethics*, XXVII, 2 (Jan. 1917), pp. 252–54.
"Eeldrop and Appleplex, I." *Little Review*, IV, 1 (May 1917), pp. 7–11.
"The Letters of J. B. Yeats." *Egoist*, IV, 6 (July 1917), pp. 89–90.
rev. R. G. Collingwood, *Religion and Philosophy. International Journal of Ethics*, XXVII, 4 (July 1917), pp. 89–90.
"The Noh and the Image." *Egoist*, IV, 7 (Aug. 1917), pp. 102–3.
"Eeldrop and Appleplex, II." *Little Review*, IV, 5 (Sept. 1917), pp. 16–19.
"Reflections on Contemporary Poetry" (IV). *Egoist*, IV, 8 (Sept. 1917), pp. 118–19.
"William James on Immortality." *New Statesman*, IX, 231 (Sept. 8, 1917), p. 547.
"Turgenev." *Egoist*, IV, 11 (Dec. 1917), p. 167.

1918

"In Memory of Henry James." *Egoist*, V, 1 (Jan. 1918), pp. 1–2.
rev. Edith Wharton, *Summer. Egoist*, V, 1 (Jan. 1918), p. 10.
"Style and Thought" (rev. Bertrand Russell, *Mysticism and Logic*). *Nation*, XXII, 25 (Mar. 23, 1918), pp. 768–69.
"Observations." *Egoist*, V, 5 (May 1918), pp. 69–70.
"Contemporanea." *Egoist*, V, 6 (June/July 1918), pp. 84–85.
"Shorter Notices" (contains rev. W. B. Yeats, *Per amica silentia lunae*). *Egoist*, V, 6 (June/July 1918), p. 87.
"The Hawthorne Aspect [of Henry James]." *Little Review*, V, 4 (Aug. 1918), pp. 47–53.
"Tarr." *Egoist*, V, 8 (Sept. 1918), pp. 10–14.
"Studies in Contemporary Criticism" (I). *Egoist*, V, 9 (Oct. 1918), pp. [113]–14.

1919

"The New Elizabethans and the Old." *Athenaeum*, 4640 (Apr. 4, 1919), pp. 134–36.
"Kipling Redivivus." *Athenaeum*, 4645 (May 9, 1919), pp. 297–98.
"A Sceptical Patrician" (rev. *The Education of Henry Adams*). *Athenaeum*, 4647 (May 23, 1919), pp. 361–62.
"Beyle and Balzac." *Athenaeum*, 4648 (May 30, 1919), pp. 392–93.
"Reflections on Contemporary Poetry" (IV). *Egoist*, VI, 3 (July 1919), pp. 39–40.
"Hamlet and His Problems." *Athenaeum*, 4665 (Sept. 26, 1919), pp. 940–41.
"The Preacher as Artist" (Donne). *Athenaeum*, 4674 (Nov. 28, 1919), pp. 1252–53.
"'The Duchess of Malfi' at the Lyric: and Poetic Drama." *Art and Letters*, III, 1 (Winter [1919/] 1920), pp. 36–39.

1920

"Modern Tendencies in Poetry." *Shama'a* (Urur, Adjar, India), I, 1 (Apr. 1920), pp. [9]–18.

"The Poetic Drama" (rev. M. Murry, *Cinnamon and Angelica*). *Athenaeum,* 4698 (May 14, 1920), pp. 635–36.

1921

"The Romantic Englishman, the Comic Spirit, and the Function of Criticism" (with "The Lesson of Baudelaire," under the heading "Notes on Current Letters"). *Tyro,* I ([Spring 1921]), p. 4.
"Prose and Verse." *Chapbook,* 22 (Apr. 1921), pp. [448]–53.
"London Letter" (II). *Dial,* LXX, 6 (June 1921), pp. [686]–91.
"London Letter" (III). *Dial,* LXXI, 2 (Aug. 1921), pp. [213]–17.
"London Letter" (IV). *Dial,* LXXI, 4 (Oct. 1921), pp. [452]–55.

1922

"London Letter" (V). *Dial,* LXXII, 5 (May 1922), pp. [510]–13.
"London Letter" (VI). *Dial,* LXXIII, 1 (July 1922), pp. [94]–96.
"London Letter" (VII). *Dial,* LXXIII, 3 (Sept. 1922), pp. [329]–31.

1923

"Dramatis Personae." *The Criterion,* I, 3 (Apr. 1923), pp. 303–6.
"John Donne." *Nation and Athenaeum,* XXXIII, 10 (June 9, 1923), p. 331–32.
"Andrew Marvell." *Nation and Athenaeum,* XXXIII, 26 (Sept. 29, 1923), p. 809.
"The Beating of a Drum." *Nation and Athenaeum,* XXXIV, 1 (Oct. 6, 1923), pp. 11–12.
"Ulysses, Order, and Myth." *Dial,* LXXV, 5 (Nov. 1923), pp. [480]–83.
"Marianne Moore." *Dial,* LXXV, 6 (Dec. 1923), pp. [594]–97.

1924

"A Prediction in Regard to Three English Authors" (Henry James, J. G. Frazer, F. H. Bradley). *Vanity Fair,* XXI, 6 (Feb. 1924), pp. 29, 98.
"A Commentary." *The Criterion,* II, 7 (Apr. 1924), pp. 231–35.

1925

"Wanley and Chapman." *Times Literary Supplement,* 1250 (Dec. 31, 1925), p. 907.

1926

"A Popular Shakespeare." *Times Literary Supplement,* 1255 (Feb. 4, 1926), p. 76.
"Chaucer's 'Troilus.'" *Times Literary Supplement,* 1281 (Aug. 19, 1926), p. 547.
"A Commentary." *The Criterion,* IV, 4 (Oct. 1926), pp. 713–18.

1927

"A Note on Poetry and Belief." *Enemy,* I (Jan. 1927), pp. 15–17.
"Literature, Science, and Dogma" (rev. I. A. Richards, *Science and Poetry*). *Dial,* LXXXII, 3 (Mar. 1927), pp. 239–43.
"A Study of Marlowe." *Times Literary Supplement,* 1309 (Mar. 3, 1927), p. 140.
"Mr. Middleton Murry's Synthesis." *The Criterion,* VI, 4 (Oct. 1927), pp. 340–47.

1928

"Isolated Superiority" (rev. Pound, *Personae*). *Dial*, LXXXIV, 1 (Jan. 1928), pp. [4]–7.
"An Emotional Unity" (rev. von Hügel's *Letters*). *Dial*, LXXXIV, 2 (Feb. 1928), pp. [109]–12.
"The Oxford Jonson." *Dial*, LXXXV, 1 (July 1928), pp. [65]–68.
Letter on *Coriolanus*, with two others under heading "Questions of Prose." *Times Literary Supplement*, 1391 (Sept. 27, 1928), p. 687.
"Elizabeth and Essex." *Times Literary Supplement*, 1401 (Dec. 6, 1928), p. 959.

1929

"The Tudor Translators." *The Listener*, I, 22 (June 12, 1929), pp. 833–34.
"The Prose of the Preacher: The Sermons of Donne." *The Listener*, II, 25 (July 3, 1929), pp. 22–23.

1930

"Poetry and Propaganda." *Bookman*, LXX, 6 (Feb. 1930), pp. 595–602.
"Thinking in Verse: A Survey of Early Seventeenth-Century Poetry." *The Listener*, III, 61 (Mar. 12, 1930), pp. [441]–43.
"The Devotional Poets of the Seventeenth Century: Donne, Herbert, Crashaw." *The Listener*, III, 63 (Mar. 26, 1930), pp. 552–53.

1935

"Audiences, Producers, Plays, Poets." *New Verse*, 18 (Dec. 1935), pp. 3–4.

1936

"Mr. Murry's Shakespeare." *The Criterion*, XV, 61 (July 1936), pp. 708–10.
"The Need for Poetic Drama." *The Listener*, XVI, 411 (Nov. 25, 1936), pp. 994–95.

1937

"The Lion and the Fox" (W. Lewis). *Twentieth Century Verse*, 6/7 (Nov./Dec. 1937), pp. [6–9].

1941

"'The Duchess of Malfy.'" *The Listener*, XXVI, 675 (Dec. 18, 1941), pp. 825–26.

1949

"The Aims of Poetic Drama." *Adam*, XVII, 200 (Nov. 1949), pp. 10–16.

1950

"Shakespeares Verskunst." *Der Monat*, II, 20 (May 1950), pp. 198–207.

Secondary Works

Articles

Askin, Denise T. "*The Waste Land*'s Missing Hanged Man: A Source in *The Tempest*." *English Language Notes,* XVIII, 2 (Dec. 1980), pp. 130–31.

Bhattacharya, Debriprasad. "T. S. Eliot on Shakespeare." *Quest,* 50 (July/Sept. 1966), pp. 45–54.

Blum, Margaret Morton. "The *Fool* in 'The Lovesong of J. Alfred Prufrock.'" *Modern Language Notes,* LXXII, 6 (June 1957), pp. 424–26.

Cameron, Elspeth. "T. S. Eliot's 'Marina': An Exploration." *Queens Quarterly,* LXXVII, 2 (Summer 1970), pp. 180–89.

Fleissner, Robert F. "'Prufrock,' Pater and Richard II: Retracing a Denial of Princeship." *American Literature,* XXXVIII, 1 (Mar. 1966), pp. 120–23.

———. "Prufrock's Ricardian Posture." *Research Studies,* XLVII, 1 (Summer 1972), pp. 41–43.

Fussell, Paul, Jr. "A Note on 'The Hollow Men.'" *Modern Language Notes,* LXV, 4 (Apr. 1950), pp. 254–55.

Gardner, Helen. "Shakespeare in the Age of Eliot." *Times Literary Supplement,* 3243 (Apr. 23, 1964), pp. 335–36.

Gleckner, Robert F. "Eliot's 'The Hollow Men' and Shakespeare's *Julius Caesar.*" *Modern Language Notes,* LXXV, 1 (Jan. 1960), pp. 26–28.

Green, Gayle. "Shakespeare's *Tempest* and Eliot's *Waste Land:* 'What the Thunder Said.'" *Orbis Litterarum,* XXXIV, 4 (1929, no month given), pp. 287–300.

Hunter, G. K. "T. S. Eliot and the Creation of a Symbolist Shakespeare." Brower, Reuben, ed., *Twentieth-Century Literature in Retrospect,* Cambridge, Mass.: Harvard University Press, 1971, pp. 191–204.

Krause, Sidney J. "Hollow Men and False Horses." *Texas Studies in Literature and Language,* II, 3 (Autumn 1960), pp. 368–77.

Major, John A. "Eliot's 'Gerontion' and *As You Like It.*" *Modern Language Notes,* LXXIV, 1 (Jan. 1959), pp. 28–31.

Marcus, Phillip L. "T. S. Eliot and Shakespeare." *Criticism,* XI, 1 (Winter 1967), pp. 63–79.

Milward, Peter. "Shakespeare in *The Waste Land.*" Milward and Anzai, Tetsuo, ed., *Poetry and Drama in the Age of Shakespeare,* Tokyo: Renaissance Institute, 1982, pp. 218–26.

Muir, Kenneth. "Changing Interpretations of Shakespeare." Ford, Boris, ed., *The Age of Shakespeare,* 1955, repr. Baltimore: Penguin Books, 1968, pp. 282–301.

Schuchard, Ronald. "T. S. Eliot as an Extension Lecturer," two-part article. *Review of English Studies,* XXV, 98 (May 1974), pp. 163–73; 99 (Aug. 1974), pp. 292–304.

Schwalb, Harry M. "Eliot's 'A Game of Chess.'" *The Explicator,* XI, 6 (Apr. 1953), item 46.

Seiler, Robert. "Prufrock and Hamlet." *English,* XXI, 110 (Summer 1972), pp. 41–43.

Tamplin, Ronald. "*The Tempest* and *The Waste Land.*" *American Literature,* XXXIX, 3 (Nov. 1967), pp. 352–72.

Torrens, James, S. J. "Eliot's Poetry and the Incubus of Shakespeare." *Thought,* LII, 207 (Dec. 1977), pp. 407–21.

———. "T. S. Eliot and Shakespeare: 'This Music Crept By.'" *Bucknell Review,* XIX, 1 (Spring 1971), pp. 77–96.

Watson, C. B. "T. S. Eliot and the Interpretation of Shakespearean Tragedy in Our Time." *Etudes anglaises,* XVII, 4 (Oct.–Dec., 1964), pp. 502–21.

Ph.D. Dissertations

Marathe, Sudhakar. "T. S. Eliot's Shakespeare Criticism: Discovery and Advance." Ph.D. Diss., University of Western Ontario, 1982.

Wilson, Gary H. "The Shakespearean Design of T. S. Eliot's Poetry." Ph.D. Diss., Temple University, 1973.

Books

Ackroyd, Peter. *T. S. Eliot: A Life.* New York: Simon and Schuster, 1984.

Allan, Mowbray. *T. S. Eliot's Impersonal Theory of Poetry.* Lewisburg, Penn.: Bucknell University Press, 1974.

Archer, William. *The Old Drama and the New.* London: Heinemann, 1923.

Baker, George Pierce. *The Development of Shakespeare as a Dramatist.* N.Y.: Macmillan, 1907.

Bethell, S. L. *Shakespeare and the Popular Dramatic Tradition.* 1944, repr. N.Y.: Octagon Books, 1977.

Bradbrook, M. C. *Themes and Conventions of Elizabethan Tragedy.* Cambridge: Cambridge University Press, 1935.

Bradley, A. C. *A Miscellany.* London: Macmillan, 1929.

————. *Shakespearean Tragedy.* 1904, repr. Greenwich, Conn.: Fawcett Books, 1966.

Bush, Ronald. *T. S. Eliot: A Study in Character and Style.* N.Y. and Oxford: Oxford University Press, 1983.

Cavell, Stanley, *The Claim of Reason.* Oxford and N.Y.: Oxford University Press, 1979.

————. *Themes out of School.* San Francisco: North Point Press, 1984.

Coleridge, S. T. *Coleridge's Miscellaneous Criticism,* ed. T. M. Raysor. Cambridge, Mass.: Harvard University Press, 1936.

Cornford, Francis Macdonald. *The Origin of Attic Comedy.* 1914, repr., ed. with a foreword and additional notes by Theodore H. Gaster, N.Y.: Doubleday, 1961.

Eastman, Arthur M. *A Short History of Shakespearean Criticism.* N.Y.: Random House, 1968.

Fluchère, Henri. *Shakespeare and the Elizabethans.* 1953 English version, repr. N.Y.: Hill and Wang, 1969.

Frye, Northrop. *T. S. Eliot.* N.Y.: Grove Press, 1963.

Gordon, Lyndall. *Eliot's Early Years.* Oxford and N.Y.: Oxford University Press, 1977.

Granville-Barker, Harley. *On Poetry in Drama.* London: Sidgwick and Jackson, 1937.

————. *Prefaces to Shakespeare.* Collected, Princeton: Princeton University Press, 1946–47.

Gray, Piers. *T. S. Eliot's Intellectual and Poetic Development, 1910–1922.* Brighton, England: Harvester Press and Atlantic Highlands, N.J.: Humanities Press, 1982.

Halliday, F. E. *Shakespeare and His Critics.* London: Gerald Duckworth, 1949.

Harrison, Jane Ellen. *Ancient Art and Ritual.* 1913, repr. Westport, Conn.: Greenwood Press, 1969.

————. *Themis.* Cambridge: Cambridge University Press, 1912.

Howarth, Herbert. *Notes on Some Figures behind T. S. Eliot.* Boston: Houghton Mifflin, 1964.

Knight, G. Wilson. *The Crown of Life.* 1947, repr. London: Methuen, 1966.

————. *The Imperial Theme.* 1931, repr. London: Methuen, 1965.

————. *The Shakespearian Tempest.* 1932, repr. London: Methuen, 1953.

————. *The Wheel of Fire.* 1930, repr. London, Methuen, 1960.

Knights, L. C. *Explorations.* 1946, repr. Harmondsworth, England: Penguin, 1964.

Leavis, F. R. *The Common Pursuit.* 1952, repr. London: Chatto and Windus, 1972.

————. *New Bearings in English Poetry.* 1932, repr. Ann Arbor: University of Michigan Press, 1964.

Lewis, Wyndham. *The Lion and the Fox.* 1927, repr. London: Methuen, 1966.

Lobb, Edward. *T. S. Eliot and the Romantic Critical Tradition.* London: Routledge, 1981.

Matthiessen, F. O. *The Achievement of T. S. Eliot.* Boston: Houghton Mifflin, 1935.

Moody, A. D. *Thomas Stearns Eliot: Poet.* Cambridge: Cambridge University Press, 1979.

————, ed. *"The Waste Land" in Different Voice.* London: Edward Arnold, 1974.

Quillian, William H. *"Hamlet" and the New Poetic: James Joyce and T. S. Eliot*. Ann Arbor: UMI Research Press, 1983.

Ralli, Augustus. *A History of Shakepearean Criticism*, two vols. London: Oxford University Press, 1932.

Robertson, J. M. *The Problem of "Hamlet."* 1919, repr. N.Y.: Harcourt, Brace, and Howe, 1920.

Santayana, George. *Essays in Literary Criticism*, ed. Irving Singer. N.Y.: Scribner's, 1956.

Smith, Carol H. *T. S. Eliot's Dramatic Theory and Practice*. Princeton: Princeton University Press, 1963.

Smith, Grover. *T. S. Eliot's Poetry and Plays: A Study in Sources and Meaning*, second ed. Chicago and London: University of Chicago Press, 1974.

Soldo, John J. *The Tempering of T. S. Eliot*. Ann Arbor: UMI Research Press, 1983.

Speaight, Robert. *William Poel and the Elizabethan Revival*. Cambridge, Mass.: Harvard University Press, 1954.

Still, Colin. *Shakespeare's Mystery Play: A Study of "The Tempest."* London: Cecil Parker, 1921.

Stoll, Elmer Edgar. *Hamlet: An Historical and Comparative Study*. Minneapolis: University of Minnesota, 1919.

Styan, J. L. *The Shakespeare Revolution: Criticism and Performance in the Twentieth Century*. Cambridge: Cambridge University Press, 1977.

Tate, Allen, ed. *T. S. Eliot: The Man and His Work*. N.Y.: Delacorte Press, 1966.

Traversi, D. A. *An Approach to Shakespeare*. London: Sands and Co., 1938.

Yeats, William Butler. *Collected Works,* vol. 4 (contains the *Samhain* writings). Stratford-on-Avon: Shakespeare Head Press, 1908.

Bibliographies

Gallup, Donald. *T. S. Eliot: A Bibliography*. London: Faber and Faber, 1969.

Martin, Mildred. *A Half-Century of Eliot Criticism*. Lewisburg, Penn.: Bucknell University Press, 1972.

Ricks, Beatrice. *T. S. Eliot: A Bibliography of Secondary Works*. Metuchen, N.J. and London: Scarecrow Press, 1980.

Index